SHORT CUTS

INTRODUCTIONS TO FILM STUDIES

OTHER TITLES IN THE SHORT CUTS SERIES

THE HORROR GENRE: FROM BEELZEBUB TO BLAIR WITCH   Paul Wells

THE STAR SYSTEM: HOLLYWOOD'S PRODUCTION OF POPULAR IDENTITIES   Paul McDonald

SCIENCE FICTION CINEMA: FROM OUTERSPACE TO CYBERSPACE   Geoff King and Tanya Krzywinska

EARLY SOVIET CINEMA: INNOVATION, IDEOLOGY AND PROPAGANDA   David Gillespie

READING HOLLYWOOD: SPACES AND MEANINGS IN AMERICAN FILM   Deborah Thomas

DISASTER MOVIES: THE CINEMA OF CATASTROPHE   Stephen Keane

THE WESTERN GENRE: FROM LORDSBURG TO BIG WHISKEY   John Saunders

PSYCHOANALYSIS AND CINEMA: THE PLAY OF SHADOWS   Vicky Lebeau

COSTUME AND CINEMA: DRESS CODES IN POPULAR FILM   Sarah Street

MISE-EN-SCÈNE: FILM STYLE AND INTERPRETATION   John Gibbs

NEW CHINESE CINEMA: CHALLENGING REPRESENTATIONS   Sheila Cornelius with Ian Haydn Smith

SCENARIO: THE CRAFT OF SCREENWRITING   Tudor Gates

ANIMATION: GENRE AND AUTHORSHIP   Paul Wells

WOMEN'S CINEMA: THE CONTESTED SCREEN   Alison Butler

BRITISH SOCIAL REALISM: FROM DOCUMENTARY TO BRIT GRIT   Samantha Lay

FILM EDITING: THE ART OF THE EXPRESSIVE   Valerie Orpen

AVANT-GARDE FILM: FORMS, THEMES AND PASSIONS   Michael O'Pray

PRODUCTION DESIGN: ARCHITECTS OF THE SCREEN   Jane Barnwell

NEW GERMAN CINEMA: IMAGES OF A GENERATION   Julia Knight

EARLY CINEMA: FROM FACTORY GATE TO DREAM FACTORY   Simon Popple and Joe Kember

MUSIC IN FILM: SOUNDTRACKS AND SYNERGY   Pauline Reay

FEMINIST FILM STUDIES: WRITING THE WOMAN INTO CINEMA   Janet McCabe

MELODRAMA: GENRE STYLE SENSIBILITY   John Mercer and Martin Shingler

NEW DIGITAL CINEMA: REINVENTING THE MOVING IMAGE   Holly Willis

FILM AND PHILOSOPHY: IMAGES OF WISDOM   Adrian Page

THE MUSICAL: RACE, GENDER AND PERFORMANCE   Susan Smith

FILM PERFORMANCE

FROM ACHIEVEMENT TO APPRECIATION

ANDREW KLEVAN

WALLFLOWER

LONDON and NEW YORK

A Wallflower Paperback

First published in Great Britain in 2005 by
Wallflower Press
4th Floor, 26 Shacklewell Lane, London E8 2EZ
www.wallflowerpress.co.uk

A catalogue record for this book is available from the British Library

ISBN 1 904764 24 X

Book Design by Rob Bowden Design

Printed in Great Britain by Antony Rowe Ltd, Chippenham, Wiltshire

CONTENTS

ACKNOWLEDGEMENTS

This book has emerged from my teaching in the Department of Film Studies within the School of Drama, Film and Visual Arts at the University of Kent. It would not have been possible without the support of the Department, the School and the University. I am privileged to work with stimulating and enlightened colleagues, and I am grateful to them for encouraging my teaching and writing. The Arts and Humanities Research Board enabled this project to be completed in a happy and civilised manner; thank you for your generosity and trust. Thank you John Gibbs for providing the opportunity to teach some of the material outside the University of Kent at the London College of Printing. Thank you Wallflower Press, and Yoram Allon in particular, for enthusiastically embracing the project, and thank you for your patience in waiting for it. William Rothman, Edward Klevan and Vivienne Penglase all suggested invaluable refinements to the text. I am heartened by the encouragements of William Rothman, and also of Stanley Cavell, V. F. Perkins and Douglas Pye. I owe a lot to the love and support of my brother and sister, Edward and Olivia, whose intensity and integrity are a wonder. My partner Vivienne is '*yar*'. I acknowledge some of my students specifically in the course of the text, but many more enhanced and invigorated the work in the seminar room. The quality of their engagement is my healthiest reassurance.

This book is dedicated to the memory of my mother and father.

PREFACE

There is a field of film commentary that examines performers as 'stars' and assesses their significance from a range of contexts and cultures – fandom, economics, technology, studio strategy and publicity. Another field, not quite as mined, places the emphasis on 'acting', exploring, for example, the influence of the Melodramatic, Vaudeville (or Music Hall), Continental Cabaret, Stanislavsky or Method techniques. Both these fields draw on external evidence to assess a performer's effect, but they tend not to pursue the complexity of a performer's internal relationships within a film. This book places the emphasis differently, treating performance as an internal element of style in synthesis with other aspects of film style and explores the achievement of expressive rapport. Film scholars often remark that developed and involved accounts of performance are difficult to write and it is hoped that this approach, with its attention to the place of performance within a network of relationships, will help critics and students to be thorough and expansive.

The Introduction sets out the conceptual underpinning, and draws attention to writing that is vivid and exemplary. Each of the three main chapters is devoted to a different aspect of synthesis: position and perspective (the relationship of the performer to the camera, and their position within the shot); place (the relationship of the performer to location, decor, furniture and objects); and plot (the relationship of the performer to narrative developments). Each chapter corresponds loosely to a genre – comedy, melodrama and thriller respectively – which allows for coherence of theme and tone. All the sequences have been chosen because they are exemplary in presenting a particular aspect or aspects of the performers' relationships. In many cases, the sequences are from films – *City Lights*, *The Music Box*, *Sons of the Desert*, *The Scarlet Empress*, *The Awful Truth*, *The Philadelphia Story*, *Shadow of a Doubt* – which have long been studied and appreciated, inside and outside the academy, and some are landmarks of the cinema. That these films may once again be invigorated is testament to their richness, but also to the value of the approach.

This book concentrates on films from the 'Golden Age' of Hollywood because they consistently, yet unassumingly, achieve an expressive rapport between performer and surroundings. An important context for the book is the recent work on interpreting 'Golden Age' Hollywood film by writers such as Stanley Cavell, V. F. Perkins, William Rothman and George M. Wilson. This body of scholarship does not simply provide accounts, or interpretations, of Hollywood films. It demonstrates how the films instruct us in ways of interpretation and ways of viewing. Because the films wish us to take responsibility for coming to moments and meanings in particular ways, they may hide their best view of themselves. Stanley Cavell's work emphasises the apparent simplicity or 'ordinariness' of Hollywood films that obscures their significance. George M. Wilson elucidates how the films develop careful visual or aural patterns that open up alternative lines of viewing, but these alternatives are deliberately less salient than, for example, the straightforward dynamics of plot. Although it focuses on films from outside Hollywood, my previous book, *Disclosure of the Everyday: Undramatic Achievement in Narrative Film*, is concerned with how apparently unimportant, uneventful or mundane elements of films – aspects of the everyday – may remain undramatic and yet, because of their arrangement within a film, unexpectedly reveal a wealth of significance. Further developing this line of thought, *Film Performance: From Achievement to Appreciation* illustrates how interpretations mature when one responds to the performer's multifaceted relationships – not always prominent – to the surrounding dramatic environment. We may well be rewarded for concentrating on a performer as they *merely* turn a street corner, sit in a chair, touch a wall, move around a bedroom or carry a bunch of flowers. Fresh aspects of even familiar films emerge when we attend to gestures, postures, expressions and voice – and how they are situated. Interpretations unfold and complicate with our moment-by-moment experience of viewing the performer's activity.

INTRODUCTION: INTERPRETING PERFORMANCE

In the entry on Fred Astaire in his 'A Biographical Dictionary of the Cinema', David Thomson writes:

> How evocative that name is: run the parts together and the result is as rhythmic as Frenesi; separate them and it could be Fred a Star or Fred on a staircase, astride the stair – thus Astaire, *l'esprit d'escalier*. It is proper to respond to in this way because so much of Astaire is a matter of stylish carriage, and I do not think it accidental that the name evokes some specially serene agility. This leads to the questions, is Astaire a movie actor? and what makes for great acting in the cinema? There is a good case for arguing that, in the event of a visit by creatures from a far universe, ignorant of the cinema, one would do best to show them some steps by Astaire as the clinching evidence of the medium's potential ... Astaire is the most refined human expression of the musical, which is in turn the extreme manifestation of pure cinema: the lifelike presentation of human beings in magical, dreamlike, and imaginary situations. (1995: 28–9)

Astaire preferred wide shots, rarely allowing the camera to separate the various parts of his body from each other – his 'lifelike presentation' – or separate him from the locale in which he moved – his 'imaginary situation'. Furthermore, Thomson writes that he was eager to 'perform in uninterrupted setups' (1995: 28). He draws attention to a moment in *Silk*

Stockings (Rouben Mamoulian, 1957) just before Cyd Charisse and Fred Astaire 'dance across several deserted film sets':

> Before the dancing begins, there is a prelude. Charisse arrives by car at the studio gates and Astaire, muttering 'Hallo, hallo...', hobbles over to meet her. That movement ... was exquisite, original, and Astaire. The emotion of the moment – of lovers reunited – hardly seems to strike him. But ask him to move from A to B and he is aroused. This touches on a vital principle: that it is often preferable to have a movie actor who moves well than one who 'understands' the part ... very few men or women can move well in front of a camera. In *The Big Sleep*, there are numerous shots of Bogart simply walking across rooms: they draw us to the resilient alertness of his screen personality as surely as the acid dialogue. Bogart's lounging freedom captures our hopes. With Astaire this effect is far more concentrated, because it is his single asset. (1995: 29)

It is indicative here that Thomson refers to Astaire and Charisse rather than to the names of the particular parts that they play. Musicals, where characters are performers of song and dance, bare the fact that characters are simultaneously performers on film. Although we have a sense of this simultaneity in all film genres, we commonly refer to a particular Astaire routine in this or that musical and we are not especially interested in the name of the character that he plays. Thomson refers to the 'exquisite' skill of Astaire's routine, and responds to the particular aspects of this achievement. Musicals provide the starkest reminder that our engagement with a performer's art is as important as our identification with a character. Moreover, rather than his skill in interpreting the part, Thomson draws out the quality of Astaire's movement within this location. This is Astaire's route into meaningful expression, for although it may be true that 'the emotion of the moment', preconceived, 'hardly seems to strike him', nevertheless his actual movement within this specific space enables him to 'strike' the emotion of (these) 'lovers reunited'.

Elsewhere, Thomson claims that a measure of screen acting is the degree of comfort with which the performer's body moves within a real space:

> The most effective actors and actresses in the cinema are those who can achieve such a degree of external and internal relaxation while being filmed that the camera records their nature without defining it ... This hypothesis is another way of repeating that the camera's recording powers are paramount in the cinema ... 'Actor' is not even a term appropriate to the cinema. The barrier of the screen certainly gives the impression of acting, but what we are seeing in the cinema are people. (1967: 123)

Stanley Cavell enlarges on the automatic integration of performer and space that is at the heart of cinema, drawing out two conditions of the medium:

> First, movie performers cannot project, but are projected. Second, photographs are of the world, in which human beings are not ontologically favoured over the rest of nature, in which objects are not props but natural allies (or enemies) of the human character. The first necessity – projected visibility – permits the sublime comprehensibility of Chaplin's choreography; the second – ontological equality – permits his ... relationships with Murphy beds and flights of stairs and with vases on runners on tables on rollers: the heroism of momentary survival. (1979: 37)

This book celebrates performances that do not place themselves to project, but which rather have the patience and humility, in tune with the medium's encouragements, to inhabit an appropriate place. Chapter One explores Chaplin's relationship to the camera in the final sequence of *City Lights* (Charles Chaplin, 1931), the construction of his 'visibility', and his 'ontological equality' with flowers, street corners and windowpanes. The same chapter investigates other comedy films that are not distinctively marked by a dense and rich *mise-ên-scène*, so that in these instances our attentiveness to the performers' *situation* is particularly required to appreciate the coherence of the films' shape and style.[1]

Thomson appreciates the situation where, 'There is less impression of the character being presented to us than of a meeting with a stranger in which one notices the physical actions of behaviour ... we see not an intended meaning but an alert personality' (1967: 123). The very 'being' of the actor, and his 'ontological equality', is crucial on film. Cavell understands that on film, characters have no existence apart from the particular human beings on screen, and no life apart from the particular performers who incarnate them. Character and performer are inextricably intertwined; they coalesce. In the theatre, character and performance are often thought of together precisely because they are conceived separately, hence an acknowledged dynamic between them that is an essential part of theatre. The separation of character and performer is explicitly part of theatrical expression – a practical and critical concern:

> For the stage, an actor works himself into a role; for the screen, a performer takes the role onto himself. The stage actor explores his potentialities and the possibilities of his role simultaneously; in performance these meet at a point in spiritual space – the better the performance, the deeper the point. In this respect, a role in a play is like a position in a game, say, third base: various people can play it, but the great third baseman is a man who has accepted and trained his skills and instincts most perfectly and matches them most intimately with his discoveries of the possibilities and necessities of third base. The screen performer explores his role like an attic and takes stock of his physical and temperamental endowment; he lends his being to the role and accepts only what fits; the rest is nonexistent. (1979: 27–8)

Cavell and Thomson's understanding of film performance is based on the photographic underpinning of the medium. Although this links the medium strongly to the real world, it is not a claim for unmediated realism. For Cavell, film 'holds reality before us' (1979: 189) and 'reality is freed to exhibit itself' (1979: 166). The film world has the characteristics of physical reality, but its makers have *presented* it to us: designed and moulded it with all the tools at their command. Charles Affron writes about

> the dimensions of the screen, the close-up, and the vocabulary of transformation and movement supplied by montage, framing, panning, tilting, and dollying. The richness of décor and the limitless possibilities of ambience belong to the rhetoric of the plastic arts ... Films are breathtakingly perched between the unequivocal

> reality of the photographic process and a style that is by definition magnifying, hyperbolic ... It is as if some great mannerist canvas were suddenly animated with breathing, moving, speaking creatures. (1977: 3–4)

Affron's comparison to the 'plastic arts' links with Thomson's idea that the good screen performer will have 'the willingness to see what the plastic realisation will be' (1967: 122). Good performance need not be naturalistic or understated – Affron's book on acting concentrates and celebrates the 'magnifying, hyperbolic' style of Lillian Gish, Greta Garbo and Bette Davis – but about taking full advantage of 'ontological equality', synthesising with the world of the film, with 'the richness of décor and the limitless possibilities of ambience'. A magnified performance can be at one with an intimate moment-by-moment engagement with surrounding structures. This relates to V. F. Perkins' thought that 'bold statements are refined by the pattern of detail built over and around them' (1972: 119). This sense of broad outlines being refined by more varied and complex configurations illuminates Cavell's idea that film characters, especially in Hollywood, are types that the performers fill with individuality. He writes, 'One recalls the lists of stars of every magnitude who have provided the movie camera with human subjects – individuals capable of filling its need for individualities ... whose inflections of demeanor and disposition were given full play in its projection' (1979: 35). Because many Hollywood performances are examining the 'hyperbolic', for example exploring the extremities of sentiment, the viewer need not only be absorbed, or overwhelmed, by the *character's* emotions, or 'identify' or empathise with them. The viewer may simultaneously engage with the *performer's* handling of these heightened emotional states. In Hollywood cinema, not only do (apparent) clichés of sentiment or emotionalism entertain; they are also entertained, and redeemed.

Rather than obeying verisimilitude, the credibility of performance is created out of coherence and harmony with the film's environment – including the camera and other elements 'outside' the visible fictional world – which then generates 'truthful' analogy and metaphor. For Affron, the noteworthy performers create patterns,

> ...and they relate to the patterns of their surrounding structure ... If we have no difficulty in seeing the links between young ladies

> and roses in Renaissance love lyrics, we should not be confused by Lillian Gish's turning into a lotus blossom or Garbo's merging with a bedpost. When Davis's face almost fills the frame during Herbert Marshall's death scene in *The Little Foxes* [William Wyler, 1941], dramatic art is not mimicking life ... Effective screen acting exploits ... perceptual dynamics – it not only invites and withstands the activity of our scrutiny, it mirrors the activity. It sets a standard for variation, for composition and recomposition, for sets of processes that thrive on the potential of repeatability. As our ear is trained to distinguish musical themes, their variations, and permutations in the constantly shifting framework of a sonata or a symphony, as our eye is challenged by the tension of masses in sculptured marble or chiaroscuro on canvas, so the screen actor, by the richness of his being and manner, by his comfort in photographic contexts, sets us a challenge ... These transformations are quite distinct from character impersonation and the acting out of plot information ... The benevolent processes are those that call us to participate, to savor the delight of their rhythms and rhymes, the flow of their contours. (1977: 6–7)

Central to Affron's method of appreciating performers, 'their composition and recomposition', is the 'potential of repeatability'. For Affron, 'the permanent existence of an image, even a moving one, is sufficient cause for testing its durability and examining its components' (1977: 4). More importantly, good performers are responding to the possibility within the medium of 'renewable scrutiny'. He writes in reference to Garbo:

> Her acting is of a complexity that makes it difficult to assess in the context of standard technique. Yet she herself supplies the clue in the model of concentration that we must emulate if we are to perceive her properly. Lodged within the triteness of most of her vehicles, the glamour of a pristine shell, and the authentic image of solitude she projects are areas of sentiment that are attainable if we are prepared to pitch our tension of awareness as high as that of the actress. Garbo sheds the seductive veils of the love goddess, but only for those who are willing to share her intricacies. Punished with the numbness of adoration if we are lax, we visit

> the depths of her being if we can withstand the painful intimacy of her method. Garbo often seems lost in the labyrinth of her own privacy. (1977: 8)

The close study of films and their performances, therefore, is not simply a particular method of film analysis, personally favoured; it is invited by the 'variations' and 'permutations' of the drama, by the 'intricacies' and 'richness' of the performance, and by the 'repeatability' of the medium. When we have 'pitch[ed] our tension of awareness as high as that of the actress', this studious activity does justice to our 'concentration'. Thus, the achievement of the performer and the appreciation of the viewer are united, and there is a similarity between the performer's art and the viewer's task. They mirror each other's efforts.

This book concentrates on individual scenes or sequences from films so that it may be responsive to their unfolding and 'savor the delight of their rhythms and rhymes, the flow of their contours'. Attending to the moment-by-moment movement of performers also enhances our understanding of film characterisation. It encourages us to attend to a character's physical and aural detail and reminds us, because we are prone to forget in our literary moods, of their ontological particularity in the medium of film. A living human being embodies a film character.

Attending to sequences is preferred to ranging across a performer's career, or simply extracting instances of performance from across a whole film. Such extractions miss the presentness of the performance and are in danger of 'assess[ing] in the context of standard technique'. James Naremore observes physical and aural features of screen acting, and he is one of the few writers to have encouraged us to attend to the technique of performance, but his understandings are restricted by 'context'. Too often these understandings are external to the internal 'rhythm and rhymes', and even within chapters organised around a single film, aspects of movement and gesture become detached examples, and are sometimes reductive. In a section on the performer's handling of objects he writes, 'when Katherine Hepburn [in *Holiday*, George Cukor, 1938] grows depressed and contemplates getting drunk, she grasps the stem of a champagne glass tightly, wrapping her hand around it and making a fist; thus the prop helps her to signal 'repressed' anger' (1988: 85). It is unlikely that a film as shrewd as *Holiday* would be this transparent or without irony in signalling the 'repressed'. It is more likely that the meaning and significance of this gesture is appropriated, or else adjusted or modulated by the developing behavioural and attitudinal patterns. Alternatively, the meaning of the gesture might be as straightforward as Naremore suggests, but then the instance is an inadequate example because it fails to exemplify the complexity of the relationship between performer and object in the cinema.

The vulnerability of Naremore's approach is exposed when it fails to illuminate the significance of a whole film. In *Stella Dallas* (King Vidor, 1937), Naremore claims:

> the characterisation depends to a great extent on Stella's gaudily inappropriate finery. During a moonlit walk with Stephen Dallas early in the film, she carries a wide straw hat in her hands, hiding her face behind it when she blushes or shyly biting the hatbrim; later, having married Dallas, she wears a dress with a long chiffon scarf that she nervously runs through her fingers; still later, when she visits a country club and tries to impress her daughter Laurel's rich friends, she flings an absurd foxfur around her neck in a pathetic attempt at regal dignity. Throughout, Stella's frilled or beribboned dresses, feathery hats, and clunky jewelry ... have been turned into veritable flags for her emotion. (1988: 89)

The problem here is that the film turns on whether Stella's costumes are 'inappropriate' or not – whereas Naremore assumes it – and the film is ambiguous about whether Stella's appearance at the country club is 'pathetic' or strategic (or a bewildering mixture of both). Cavell, for example, writes, 'The evidence that Stella knows her effect at the resort hotel turns simply on her massively authenticated knowledge of clothes, that she is an expert at their construction and, if you like, at their deconstruction' (1996: 201). The film – 'throughout' – is too suggestive and ambivalent about costume to allow it to be 'flags' for emotions. Even if we are in doubt about Stella's intentions at the resort hotel – indeed because we are in doubt – Barbara Stanwyck's Stella unsettles our 'veritable' judgements – possibly 'inappropriate' – about other people's clothing. Naremore, however, is dangerously close to aligning himself with the aristocratic assumptions the film pointedly places under scrutiny, and this interpretive weakness is because his writing is unresponsive, in Affron's terms, to the 'painful intimacy' of the performer's method, refusing to 'share [Stanwyck's] intricacies'.

For Cavell, although Stanwyck's Stella is 'unknown' to those around her ('Stella learns the futility of appealing to the taste of those who have no taste for her' (1992: 202)) she invites us to engage with her private sensitivities:

> [Stella's] sure knowledge of her own effect is separately authenticated in the sequence in which we see her hurriedly and surely alter a black dress in which to receive her husband Stephen [from whom she is now separated] ... The resulting, not quite basic black dress is not exactly Stella's taste ... but it certainly satisfies Stephen's. He even goes so far as to suggest, as if in response, that he and Laurel [Stella's daughter] might take a later train in order to stay and have dinner with her. But when Ed Munn barges in drunk ... Stephen takes Laurel away at once ... Stella stands in that black dress, her back to the camera, watching the closed door behind which Stephen and Laurel have disappeared. The shot is held somewhat longer than one might expect, calling attention to itself ... As elsewhere, a figure on film turned away from us tends to signal a state of self-absorption, of self-assessment, a sense of thoughts under collection in privacy. (1996: 202–3)

Cavell understands 'privacy' to be a central aspect of Hollywood performance, and in discussing *Now, Voyager* (Irving Rapper, 1942), he writes: 'The wish, in the great stars ... is a function not of their beauty, such as that may be, but of their power of privacy, of a knowing unknowness. It is a democratic claim for personal freedom. It is something [Bette] Davis shares with the greatest histrionic romantic stars, Garbo and Dietrich, sometimes Ingrid Bergman, and among American women, Barbara Stanwyck' (1996: 128). Cavell's insight suggests that a viewer's engagement with a performer depends on him or her communicating aspects of their character's consciousness. Such an understanding should remind us again that our disposition towards a narrative is not necessarily tied to our identification with character – however elegantly refined – but lies equally with appreciating the performer's capacities for revealing *and* withholding aspects of the character's sensibility. We are invited to consider – *and* be considerate of – Stella's thoughts even though we only see her from behind, indeed because we only see her from behind. (The eloquence of the moment is achieved by the performer's bearing in *conjunction* with the position of the camera.)

There is a relationship between responsiveness to performance and complexity of interpretation. Elsewhere, Cavell surrenders to the 'detail' of Irene Dunne in *The Awful Truth* (Leo McCarey, 1937) and this reveals 'what the film is about': 'my sense ... is that if one is not willing to yield to Irene Dunne's temperament, her talents, her reactions, following their detail almost to the loss of one's own identity, one will not know, and will not care, what the film is about' (1981: 233). Affron discusses Garbo's performance in *Queen Christina* (Rouben Mamoulian, 1933) and implies that we should not be blinded to the complexity of the film's meaning because of 'the treacly score' and because the 'art direction ... belongs to the usual MGM paint-and-gloss school'. Despite these aspects, he states:

> Mamoulian's patience matches Garbo's. He allows her to inhabit the film: to stand in window frames, to touch tables, to sit on a throne, and make her sitting there seem essential to the character as well as to the rank of queen ... In the inn sequence, Garbo progresses through various stages of sexual ambiguity and leads an audience to a new level of perception ... The processes of reappraisal and reinterpretation of sexual identity elicited by Garbo are then extended into a broader physical context. Her eyes, hands, and body seem to fondle a room and its objects, creating a version of a love nest for remembrance. The sense of place emanates from her oblique absorption in self. Her own image is reflected in [a] rustic mirror while she searches for [John] Gilbert's. A peculiarly mixed effect of sensuality and absence of the love object idealises sexual satisfaction with the cherishing wrappings of premature nostalgia ... Wool reintroduces texture; its softness establishes the motif for Garbo's imprint upon yielding surfaces. She slithers across the bed with an unnatural turn of the body. This turn leads into the increased focus of face upon pillow as her love for a man is evoked in the solitary contact with an object ... [Later] Garbo touches a religious picture and then consecrates the wooden bedpost with pillowlike tenderness and holy devotion. (1977: 178–82)

Affron responds to Garbo's placement and relationship with the room and furniture around her, and to their texture ('The actress is impressed into surfaces whose receptivity ranges from the hard depth of the mirror to the yielding surfaces of wool and pillow' (1977: 183)). He responds to the unfolding of posture and gesture and its *changing* relationship to the camera as the 'unnatural turn of the body ... leads into the increased focus of face upon pillow.' In addition, he responds to the rhyming of gesture that allows patterning across the sequence, so that the 'wooden bedpost', coming after wool and pillow, can now take on a 'pillowlike tenderness' ('there is a fusion of hard and soft when she applies the poles of her touch and being to the wooden bedpost' (ibid.)). Most importantly, however, Affron is alive to the 'processes of reappraisal and *reinterpretation*' [my italics] that Garbo's configurations engender. In general, he draws out the tension between Garbo's love for the presence of objects (she 'bestows her unaffected commitment upon things' (ibid.)) and her mourning for them, as if they were already lost, the 'premature nostalgia' which makes 'a love nest for remembrance'. Despite the strength of her responsiveness to place, Affron understands this to be at one with an 'absorption in self' (perhaps walking through the 'labyrinth of her own privacy'), and this interpretation is crystallised when, in the mirror, her search for Gilbert becomes a reflection of herself.

Affron illustrates how attention to performance may enhance the *density* of our interpretations because we are responsive, like Garbo in the bedroom, to physicality and texture. Taken along with the movement of the performer we are sensitive to the movement of meaning, drawn into the 'processes of reappraisal and reinterpretation'. When we 'pitch our tension of awareness as high as that of the actress', our intensity is no longer satisfied by thin interpretations based on general themes or summaries of narrative strands. Garbo's behaviour opens up intricate tensions and ambiguities because a good performer's sympathy (to surroundings) enables flexibility: they have the 'willingness to see what the plastic realisation will be'. Thomson understands the supreme screen actor to be Cary Grant and claims him 'the best and most important actor in the history of the cinema' (1995: 300):

> Grant's ... most consistent quality is a diffidence or reserve to the events of his movies which gives immediate impression of a real

> intelligence meeting those events not in a predetermined way but with a flexible novelty of experience. As the attitude attracts our interest, so the completeness of our involvement in the wide potential of his decisions reflects on our interest and thus on what, in the same circumstances, our decision might be. It is Grant's ability to suggest the embodiment of all characteristics simultaneously. The manner and outward 'style' are alert to this range but not necessarily aware of every direction it will take. (1967: 125–6)

Grant's 'real intelligence meeting those events ... with a flexible novelty of experience' links with Cavell's evocation: 'the air [Grant] can convey of mental preoccupation, of a continual thoughtfulness' (1981: 145). There is a tension between the hyperbolic environments of Hollywood – aristocratic, glamorous, decadent, shadowy, grimy or dusty – and the deftness and agility with which they are then inhabited, intelligently animated, by a 'continual thoughtfulness'.

Thomson highlights a moment in *Morocco* (Josef von Sternberg, 1930) where Marlene Dietrich, performing in cabaret, is dressed as a man and 'she gazes at [a] woman for several seconds before lightly but sensuously kissing her on the lips. The pause while she considers the gesture is not only one of the cinema's finest suspensions of the moment but an instance of Dietrich seeming to gain understanding of herself from her own actions. Within the total artificiality of von Sternberg's films this is an extraordinary freedom for the actress to retain' (1967: 112–13). Chapter Three concentrates on a particularly story-led genre, the thriller, to focus on how our appreciation of certain performances can reveal other stories that are less immediately apparent, and adjust our understanding of what is motivating a character. Thomson continues:

> There is another sequence involving the suspension of the moment. [Gary] Cooper and Dietrich have agreed to go away. He remains in her dressing-room while she goes into the café to sing. While we hear the music he wanders around the dressing-room aimlessly. He finds a necklace that Adolphe Menjou has given Dietrich and he tries on her black top hat. Then he writes, 'I changed my mind. Good Luck', on the mirror and goes back to the desert. There is much more to the sequence, of course, but none of it is conclusive.

> Cooper's reason might be anger at seeing the necklace, a sense of interior confinement, an aroused distrust of women, a passing fancy or the thought that all love is lived through and forgotten. He may not have any reason – the freedom is shocking in its destructiveness. (1967: 138)

The moment is more opaque than is characteristic in Hollywood films, but it exemplifies the performer's ability to keep alive the various options which have emerged from the world that the film has established. This suspended moment prevents us fixing our interpretations and it opens up possibilities. The performer resists asserting a single emotional response, and allows us to wonder at the different stories available to his character.

V. F. Perkins discusses the use of the long take in *The Magnificent Ambersons* (Orson Welles, 1942) and its capacity to let a moment breathe. He discusses the conversation between George (Tim Holt) and Lucy (Anne Baxter), after George's mother has given in to her son's demand that she cut off all contact with Lucy's father, Eugene (Joseph Cotton):

> Lucy seems not to have heard about this when George meets her, by chance, on a walk through town. The camera tracks them as they stroll along the boardwalk ... We may sense ... the frivolously brisk manner in which Lucy responds to his every effort to boost the importance of their relationship, that she has herself in training to cure herself of love for a man that she cannot respect. Yet her unthought impulse is betrayed (to any eyes more alert than George's) by the ease with which she falls into walking with him, sharing his pace and very soon leaning in to his shoulder in a harmony of movement at odds with her spoken attitudes. The boardwalk scene is a fine example of the subtlety that can be attained when the camera is held back from any display of psychological awareness and discrimination ... A vital aspect of Welles' long-take practice is its refusal of the easy rhetoric of emotional and psychological exposure that analytical editing makes available. In conventional practice the timing of the cuts and especially the deployment of close-up provide a means to assert the special significance of a gesture, a glance, a reaction ... It is routine to bang

> in close-ups where the drama has no valid climax and where the actor has nothing of substance on display. Welles seems to wish to dissociate himself from the notion that the camera can supply insight not achieved in performance; and his practice can be taken to reflect a recoil from an excessively easy confidence in the camera's assertion of motive and undeclared feeling. (1999: 58–9)

The actors' and the camera's behaviour are mutually considerate; each trusts the other to enhance understanding and to relieve them of the sole burden of making themselves known.

Chapter Two explores how aspects of character psychology in melodrama are indirectly revealed by the performer's relationship to other aspects of a film's presentation. This relieves the performer of the need to overtly or openly express their psychological states and betray their latent or covert aspects; instead, the performer remains faithful to the submerged quality of these emotions. Perkins continues:

> Welles ... seems to wish to limit the actors' display of the characters' drives and appetites. The likely ground for this is that the projection of the characters' motivations is liable either to place the actors in superiority to their roles or to carry the sense of the characters' awareness of the (now no longer) hidden sources of action, bestowing a rarely appropriate sense of self-understanding ... Though the visual style is as overt as Lang's or Sternberg's or Hitchcock's ... these devices are not used to construct a knowledge of character more certain or clear-cut than the knowledge we can derive from deeds and gestures. (1999: 59–61)

Perkins then goes on to substantiate his point by discussing the inappropriateness of a close-up at the end of the sequence and how it narrows its meaningful range:

> In its very last section, after George has left, the long take is punctured by a studio insert: a soft-focus close-up of a tearful Lucy. This comes to interrupt her contemplation of George's departure and to tell us how she *really* feels, by defining her private thought as against her public display. So her composure was mainly for

> George's deception, and served no significant need of her own. The insert could pose as a clarification. Then we can see that to clarify inappropriately is to change and diminish by giving us just that simple definition of Lucy's mental state that would – if we took it seriously – make her situation banal and her previous action merely stubborn. The cut into close-up carries the sense of a special truth isolated by the camera's knowing eye. Here it asks too much of the apparatus and almost nothing of the actress. It clarifies by a sudden reduction of our space for thought and wonder. (1999: 61–2)

When the film 'asks too much of the apparatus and almost nothing of the actress' we have a good example of aspects out of balance. Indeed, in *Film as Film* (1972), Perkins offers the most developed claim for synthetic coherence and its relationship to significance of meaning. He writes about the 'organisation of details whose relationships simultaneously complicate and clarify the movie's viewpoint ... the value of their interaction and the extent of their integration ... the effort to maintain the various elements in productive tension and neither to push them into symmetrical alignment ... nor to let them fall into blank contradiction' (1972: 119–20). *The Magnificent Ambersons* had opened up 'our space for thought and wonder' before, in this case, the studio thought to reduce it.

* * *

The introduction to Lesley Stern and George Kouvaros' edited collection on film performance, *Falling For You*, is entitled 'Descriptive Acts' and in it they argue for an attention to film performance not only for its own sake but as a route into greater sensitivity in the ways we describe films, where

> description is seen as something far from self-evident, or simple, but central to critical practice ... description is a *question* of how to bring into existence, how, in the course of analysis, to evoke for a reader that lost object ... Ideally we would like to write in such a way as to bring the film into imaginative being for the reader, so that she views it in the process of reading. In reading she becomes a film viewer. But we would also like to offer a persuasive inter-

> pretation based on attentiveness to the object, on detailed and accurate rendition. (1999: 7–9)

These ambitions are encouraged by the study of performance because of its desire to recover or conjure a sense of 'corporeal presence' and 'mobility' (1999: 14). (Stern and Kouvaros indirectly argue that the paucity of work on film performance is a consequence of evading this manner of writing.) Most of the writers quoted in this introduction were chosen not simply because of their insight into film performance but because their insight is inseparable from the quality of engagement with the 'presence' of the films. Furthermore, passages have been quoted at length so that the flow of their language, precisely 'recovering' the 'mobility' of performance, is reasonably unbroken. Cavell writes in his discussion of *Bringing Up Baby* (Howard Hawks, 1938) that 'nothing about our lives is more comic than the distance at which we think about them' (1981: 132). We may say that nothing about our writing on films is more comic than the distance at which we think about them: our determination to choose a set of words and arrangements – neutral, positivistic, empirical, technical, objective – that exist in a different orbit to the tone of a film's expression. Stern and Kouvaros describe this determination as a 'decided rejection of the descriptive (conceived of as always duplicitous, subjective, rhetorical, misleadingly mimetic) in favour of a turn towards a more scientific or technical language' (1999: 8). An appreciation of performance allows us a different opportunity. One of the challenges of film study is to evoke in words a medium that is primarily visual and aural, and *moving*. Stern and Kouvaros continue:

> In order to set the scene before the eyes of the reader the writer needs ... a degree of fictionalisation. This is not to turn the film into fiction; but in order to turn the film into writing, in order to convey movement, corporeal presence ... and effective inflections, a certain refiguring is required, an attentiveness to the fictional impulse at the heart of any [descriptive] endeavour. In terms of film this is not to argue for a fictionalisation and misrepresentation, but for a way of evoking rather than effacing the fictional charge. (1999: 17)

Only if we evoke the 'fictional charge' of a film will we be meeting the spirit in which the film performers move before us. Only then, during that process of evocation, will they disclose themselves with equal vivacity; and given that our effort to appreciate will forever be in process, in pursuit, there will always be more of their achievement to emerge.

1 POSITION AND PERSPECTIVE

Shifting perspectives: City Lights

The final sequence of *City Lights* (Charles Chaplin, 1931) is exact about the developing stages of the performer's exposure. Charlie the Tramp is in love with a young woman, a blind flower seller who plies her trade on the streets (Virginia Cherrill). He finds money for her so that her sight may be restored, but winds up in jail. In the final section of the film, which begins with his release, he finds her working in an up-market flower shop. After some delay, she realises who is standing before her. In the final shot of the film, his face is shown in close-up, observed by a woman whose first sight of him is at an advanced stage of their relationship.

The distinction of the final close-up is to provide a view of Charlie cut away from the surrounding environment; it is a close-up which also closes off. This contrasts to most of the shots in the film within which Chaplin carefully situates his performance. The film's scenes are often constructed so that the viewer has a more privileged perspective than the main character. *City Lights* adopts variations on the 'He's Behind You' blueprint, at its most heart-stopping when, earlier in the film, Charlie steps forward to peer at a female statue in a shop window. We view Charlie through the shop window, and part of the sidewalk directly behind him mechanically disappears (it is a goods' elevator). Charlie's hop backwards to admire the object, perfectly timed, is met by the rise of the pavement. Charlie repeats the fortuitous trick a number of times, and concern over the character's potentially drastic disappearance finds relief in the performer's flowing synchronisation with his surroundings. This type of comic construction is used throughout the final sequence but its deployment has varied and deepened. The street-elevator gag depends on Charlie looking into the pane while the viewer looks out at him, and now, within this final sequence, the flower shop window acts as an axis around which the positions of the performers and our perspective on them are exactly adjusted.[1] The effect of the construction depends on an acceptance that the film routinely and necessarily asserts a more expansive view than the one apprehended by the character. The conspicuousness is a crucial aspect to the approach because the glaring and unmistakable contrasts in point of view – between what we see and what the character sees – provide parameters within which the performer controls the unfolding of his comedy. The film encourages us to watch and locate Charlie to appreciate *Chaplin's* performance of isolation and obliviousness.

The sequence is tapered to a point where it concludes with the final close-up. It begins with a medium shot from inside the flower shop, a typically more inclusive perspective, after the inter-title 'Autumn'. This shot allows us to look on to a range of activity within the shop while at the same time being able to look beyond it, through the large glass windows, to the street outside. Because the city streets have been important locations throughout the film – the previous place of her livelihood and the meeting place with Charlie – the presence of the exterior in the shot is not merely background colouring. The expansive view also reduces the prominence of the first evidence that the woman has been cured of her blindness. In between her business, she puffs up the side of her hair in the mirror that sits upon the glass counter. Her gesture is no more than a quick check between her tasks, and it occurs within a shot that takes in other movements in the shop and outside. The performer's gesture confirms her sight but it is presented in the spirit with which it is carried out: passing and casual. It is not given the attention one might expect of a significant narrative verification, nor is it dwelt upon to inflate the sentiment.[2] We experience the young woman's regaining of sight through consequence rather than direct confirmation. Her presence in the shop interior indicates improved social circumstance, with the street now behind her; and this shot requires us to look through her present predicament to the life of the street that lies behind it.

The final close-up of Charlie does not simply contrast with previous views: equally important is the evolution of the sequence, the particular unfolding of perspective that deepens the significance of the final shot. Hence, the importance of Charlie entering scenes by turning corners: they are routine constructions of the city, endlessly tramped around, but also possible places of events where new things may come into sight (while others get left behind): where he may at last turn the corner. The flower shop is also positioned on a corner, but the film holds back this knowledge. As Charlie limps on from the right of the frame, the shop is not in shot. The following sequence, involving a battle between some newspaper boys and Charlie, takes the action, and therefore Charlie, around the corner, and brings the shop into view. One boy shoots a pea at him, and rather than exacting revenge, he resigns himself to plodding around another corner. Another pea hits him and he turns to point, but his body points in the other direction, and he continues to walk away from them. It is at this moment that, behind him, the shop comes into view, but its prominence in the shot is reduced because the emphasis remains on his reaction to being hit. The film cuts to a wider view taking in Charlie on the left of the frame and the boy on the right. The flower girl is now in the centre of the shot behind the window but because of her relative distance and her stillness in comparison to the broader movements between Charlie and the boy, the film indicates her centrality while, for the time being, muting her significance. Eruptions of physical clowning deftly regulate shifts of viewpoint.

The whole of the final sequence is infused by the sense of turning, and of turning to see, and Chaplin's comic turn involves rotating his upper body to point at the boys. Chaplin's positioning allows the film to suspend a number of different emotional possibilities: his lower body is sloping away (never to know), his upper body turns back to the boys (to be humiliated), and this fraught combination might cause him to turn fully around (to find hope). His turn towards the boys means that he fails to see an older woman sweeping discarded off-cuts who emerges from the flower shop behind him, and just before he turns his head back, she completes her task and disappears back into the shop. Because his head is dipped in regret, he does, however, catch sight of a white flower head down in the gutter, and we are presented with the other significant close-up of the sequence. Clearly, the flower stands out because it is a reminder of his love for the flower woman, but the film's concentration upon it also contrasts to the throwaway reason for its presence in the gutter: a discarded flower suddenly becomes an object of unexpected and charged meaning. Although the boy's attack may be vulgar and violent, it casts Charlie into a position that enables a delicate flower to appear miraculously under his nose. The final sequence of *City Lights* maintains a compact space within which Charlie is poised between extreme, and apparently incompatible, varieties of emotional situation and outcome.

The performer bleeds together low gags and high ideals, toppling and tenderness. The boys watch Charlie as he bends down to pick up the flower and they consequently mask any activity in the flower shop. He reaches down with one foot on the sidewalk and one foot on the road and as well as ensuring the instability of his stance, this position creates an obtrusive protrusion of his behind. Unsurprisingly, the newspaper boy snatches the opportunity, grabbing some cloth (possibly underwear, or possibly lining) through a hole in his pants. Charlie spins around, almost collapsing, and grabs back the bit of cloth. He attempts to chase the boys, and the camera moves right with him. They run off-screen right and the camera halts its movement leaving Charlie at the corner of the sidewalk and at the edge of the frame looking off-screen at the flight of the boys. This sweeping movement of Charlie and camera clears away the boys, and leaves the women in the flower shop in the centre of the frame, for the first time directly watching and laughing at Charlie's

escapades. The film then cuts to a shot that takes in both Charlie and the young woman, a shot that more acutely emphasises their proximity, and their unawareness. Charlie glances at the ripped cloth, folds it up, blows his nose on it, puts it in his top pocket, and then pats his pocket to flatten it off. Any vulgarity is redeemed by the undertaking of a polite disposal, sandwiched between the propriety of the folding and the fastidiousness of the patting, effortlessly bleeding the dirty into the dainty. The camera, by not pointing up Chaplin's folding and patting, further renders it a formality (to be observed).

His preparation of the handkerchief gently caps the manic sequence with the boys, softens the tone, and as a suitable sartorial preparation for his loved one, it delicately opens up the next stage in the drama. Indeed, his patting of his pocket appropriately triggers a shot from *inside* the shop that links him with the woman more strikingly than hitherto (the two-shot is from behind the head of the young woman and out towards Charlie). The two are in close proximity now, but the windowpane is still between them. His body faces the window, and he holds out the white flower in front of him, precariously in his fingertips. His head, however, is still turned towards the left, his eyes still fixed, presumably, on his fleeing assailants. The flower becomes a gift offered to her, presciently, before he realises her presence. This is possibly a lucky accident, but his holding out of the flower could be an indication of his readiness, and a reward for it, because he is always holding out for the woman he loves. The turn of his head towards the window, and towards her, is now charged, and the relationship between performer and camera refines the theme of blindness and sight: for example, turning to see (for Charlie), coming to see (for the flower woman) and preparing to see (for the viewer).

The two performers are now brought closer and closer together, in deliberate and careful stages. The film uses, and plays against, the convention of drawing out that inevitable end-point of the harmonious loving couple. These stages do not milk easy sentiment, for while the couple moves towards each other they find themselves in awkward and perplexing positions. The removal of each barrier permits greater intimacy but also presents new situations of suspension, culminating with the indeterminate final close-up of Charlie's face. The flower head drops to the ground; she collects a white rose and holds it out to him. From a perspective outside the shop, we see them both move left: Charlie to move on his way, the woman to the doorway. She calls to him and they hold positions at either side of the frame. The barrier of the shop window, and the axis that provided many of the complexities of perspective, is removed. The view of the drama now becomes more straightforward; we look directly at the characters as they must look directly at each other, and this marked shift in the presentation of the sequence enhances the sense of all participants (characters and viewer) suddenly vulnerable and exposed.

The physical barrier having disappeared, they must now bridge the space between them. She holds out the flower, and Charlie, without moving his position at the edge of the frame, gently rocks while outstretching his arm to collect it. The tiny flower is their pivot, and holds them in balance; what unites them is what comes between them. She then holds out a coin and wraps his hand around it. Her gift alone would be sternly ironic: an appropriate offering to a tramp, perhaps, but an inappropriate one for your benefactor. This is also the moment of her realisation, and the occasion for the film to move in and stay close. A closer shot now shows their hands wrapped together, emphasising that her touch is essential for her to see (because for so long it substituted for her sight). She moves her hand up his arm to his shoulder and the camera pans with her until Charlie's face fills the shot. The film then switches between closer shots of Charlie and views of her over his shoulder.[3] This technique of editing cuts them apart while they stand together and emphasises the separateness of their views of each other. A conventional technique of editing – over-the-shoulder shots – becomes distinct, precisely conjoined to a particular moment (rather than being an inevitable continuation, or a requirement, say, of clear syntax). Charlie's caption reads, 'You can see now?' and as she announces, 'Yes, I can see now', clutching his hand to her chest, the film cuts to that final close-up of Charlie. The close-up is not from her perspective: we view from outside their eye-line, and there is a heightened sense of watching his eyes watching her. What will she now feel, seeing him for the first time: wonder, desire, admiration, pity or disappointment? Chaplin's face catches the apprehension of all these possibilities: his dark browed eyes are worried and hopeful; and his furtively fingered mouth smiles and grimaces. The shot cuts away the trusted body of the performer: his dexterity of movement cannot rescue him. As the film moves towards this epiphany of recognition, it immobilises and humbles the great performer, suspends him as it fades out – forever at the mercy of her sight.

Simple perspectives: The Music Box and Sons of the Desert

Stan and Ollie have spent most of *The Music Box* (James Parrott, 1932) endeavouring to get a piano, encased within a wooden box, firstly up a huge flight of steps, and then into the upstairs window of a locked house. The box is now smashed, and the piano sits amongst all the debris in the lounge of the house. Stan lifts up the piano lid to have a tinkle, and Ollie comes across and gives him a violent shove. He then switches on the automatic system, and we are shown a close-up of the music roll: 'Medley of Patriotic Songs'. As the music starts to roll, Stan attempts to look inside the piano for the source of the magic. Ollie slams down the lid, and announces, 'Now let's get this place cleaned up.'

Stan moves across to the left-hand side of the frame, in front of Ollie, who is moving in the opposite direction, toward the right-hand side. Ollie's fingertips skip across the top surface of the piano, and when there is no more piano upon which to travel, they flick up into the air. Stan and Ollie have made the first moves in their dance with each other. From shoving and smashing, to dancing. Oliver Hardy and Stan Laurel show an effortless capacity to shift their moods, and shift their moods together, without contrivance, and without producing jarring contrasts in tone. Unfortunately, once the music starts playing, they not only forget all their prior difficulties but also do not realise that they are simply moving the mess from one side of the room to the other.

Their characters' capacity to forget may be childish, or childlike, but it is not infantile. Despite the monotonous futility of their tasks, they are adult enough to create an occasion for play. As they perform their playfulness for each other – with each other – they seem to be spontaneously co-ordinating their moves with casual panache.[4] We would not expect their dance movements to have specialist expertise, or virtuosity, but they achieve an enviable quality of simple improvisation, genial and convivial. In front of the piano lies a larger, flat piece of wood, the side of the box that once contained the piano, and which has escaped a shattering. It is now a raised piece of stage while the long, thin piece of wood in Stan's right hand is his cane. He does a quick piece of tap and knocks his knees together to accompany the final beats of the musical phrase (their knocking makes a loud hollow sound, as if they too were made of wood). His knocking knees are the first of four variations that accompany the conclusion of each musical phrase of the 'Patriotic Medley'. Ollie watches on from the side, and grants a turn to his partner; he then pushes his hat forward from the back of his head, and struts to the left of the frame like a clucking chicken. He now does his bit on the stage, and adopts his own embellishment with which to conclude a phrase: he raises his bent leg, and drums his fingers upon his knee, his wrist slightly cocked, with a satisfied flourish. It is one of his dainty, fiddly gestures, almost effeminate, like the skipping fingers across the piano top. Oliver Hardy allows both senses of precious to cohere in these gestures: precious in the sense of being affected, and in the sense of being valuable. His poking of his raised

knee provides a nimble and sprightly counterpoint to the crassness of the musical beat. These gestures are light of touch and they contrast with his heaviness of body, and his willingness to throw it around. When he slams his foot, for example, he interrupts and concludes a short period of tap by Stan, and injects some gusto into the third variation. Typical of the pair's fraught congruence, it brings their routine worryingly near to blunder while also providing a requisite moment of harmony: Ollie here steps in time, just in time. (Their togetherness is more straightforwardly expressed when they take their partner by the hand, as if at a barn dance, and rotate around their makeshift stage.) Ollie attempts the next turn of tap and Stan, wishing to return the favour of Ollie's stamp, slams the top of the piano, and so, on the fourth variation, raises the percussive stakes a little too high. The magical spell is broken: the piano jumps to a different tune, and Ollie jumps in fright.

The variations of gesture provide a rich variety of punch line – the lines, in this case, being musical phrases. The camera refrains from providing further emphasis: there are no close-ups of knocking knees, or stamping feet, or of pieces of wood being picked up and placed down. Crucially, the whole of this dance sequence is enacted within a shot that takes in most of the width of the room; the piano stands in the centre of the shot and they move from side to side in front of it. The shot exhibits both their charming compatibility – their mutual appreciation – and the cancelling out of each other's work (as they move the wood from one side of the room to the other). It constructs a proscenium arch that allows a stage for the success of their performance *and* allows us to monitor the failure of their progress. The shot generously includes, and permits us to view, all variations of their synchronisation, while the edges of the frame act as the borders, or boundaries, of a space where they are contained, inevitably turning back to counteract. They are attuned to everything except the failure of their task, creating poise while they destroy purpose.

Rhythm, achieved by carefully timing the interaction of elements, is crucial to all the great film performers, but Laurel and Hardy's distinction was to make their coupling the heart of their cadences. In this musical sequence from *The Music Box*, Stan and Ollie's rhythms of interaction are declared in the form of a dance. Usually their symbiotic rhythms are less prominent, but underpin other comic activity. Rhythm provides coherence to the succession of chaotic acts. Laurel and Hardy's build up and development of a gag sequence construct an effective framework and their reactions and responses to the ongoing events shrewdly vary tone and pace. Crucially, however, the performers' reciprocation of posture and gesture deepens the achievement because their rhythmic understanding conveys indirect aspects of human association.

Unlike this dance sequence, therefore, they mostly fail to acknowledge moments where they are in tune, while they dwell upon all their discordant noises. In *Sons of the Desert* (William A. Seiter, 1933) they arrive home from a convention that their wives have forbidden them to attend. They are supposed to be returning from Ollie's convalescence in Honolulu. Unfortunately, the ship sailing from Honolulu has sunk, and their wives have gone to find news of their whereabouts. Fearing their demise, and taking solace at a movie house, their wives watch a newsreel story about the convention. They see Stan and Ollie in the newsreel and, sure enough, the boys are gleefully waving and smiling to the camera, like kids sending greetings to the folks back home!

After tripping over suitcases and pricking themselves on pineapples, Stan and Ollie sit down at the table, on which Ollie taps his fingers with impatience and anxiety. He taps out a basic rhythm, and an apparently peripheral and unconnected action – Stan placing his hat down on the table – is perfectly timed to cause the sound that produces the final beat. Inquiring about his wife, Ollie asks 'I wonder where she is?' and Stan replies, 'Maybe she went out.' Ollie replies with exasperation, 'I know she went out, but what I'd like to know is, where did she *went*?' While chastising Stan for stating the obvious, Ollie makes a glaring grammatical mistake, but this itself is too conspicuous to adequately account for the humour. 'Go' may be the correct usage, but 'went' is more appropriate to the rhythm of his speech – and to their exchange: it completes the repetition of 'went' ('Maybe she *went* out', 'I know she *went* out', 'where did she *went*'), and cannot avoid crowning the welter of 'w's ('wonder', 'where', 'went', 'kno*w*', 'went', 'what', 'kno*w*', and 'where'). As Hardy vocally accentuates the final 'went', he also nods his head and jabs his finger, enhancing and justifying the fluency of his rhythm while further impressing his clumsiness.

The boys attempt to sleep in the roof (like 'two peas in a po*d*' according to Ollie, rather than 'two peas in a pot' as Stan would have it), but one fine mess leads to another. A policeman (a familiar figure of authority in Stan and Ollie's world) forces them to face their wives, soaking wet, in nightclothes and bowler hats. There then follows a complex piece of comedy performance, and the complexity is enabled by a straightforward use of the camera. A medium shot shows Stan and Ollie sitting next to each other on the sofa, while their wives wait to see which of their husbands will be forthcoming with the truth. Ollie looks forward out of the frame and points out to the distance: 'We were sailing along in clear weather, when all of a sudden a terrible storm came up – didn't it Stanley?' 'Yes', confirms Stan, 'and then we floundered in a typhoid.' Ollie is forced to correct Stan's imperfect rhyme: 'Not typhoid. He means typhoon, sugar.' He resumes the story with an excited tone: 'Then the ship started to sink and we both dived overboard', his hands miming a diving motion as he says 'overboard', and then turns once again for confirmation, 'Didn't we Stanley?' Rather than providing simple confirmation, Stan is taken with the dramatic force of Ollie's suspenseful story: 'Yes. Just as the boat was going down for the third time!' Ollie doesn't need Stan to help him with the story, indeed Stan continues to confuse it, but Ollie cannot operate without him. The film cuts away at this point to Ollie's wife who informs him that the rescue ship with the survivors does not return until tomorrow, and then cuts back to the continuation of their defence. Ollie puts one leg over the other and holds a book. Stan says: 'Must have got there after we left.' Delighted with Stan's explanation Ollie repeats his words as if they were singing a song together 'That's right. It must have got there after we left. Thank you Stanley.' ('You're welcome', responds Stan graciously.) It is apt that the wives hover on the edges of the frame, *looking down* upon the seated Stan and Ollie, while the boys sit side by side and look to each other to (create) help. Every failure in their world (in front of others, beneath others) is at the same time an achievement of imagination and intimacy (with each other).

The creative interplay is disclosed through intimacy of gesture, hence the physical significance of *Stanley*'s final re-introduction. After Stan explains that they 'ship-hiked', and Ollie is forced to continue the tale – 'yes, we thumbed our way' – while enhancing it with the appropriate (thumbing) gesture, he is then forced by his wife to expand. He continues his breathtaking reconstruction by pointing off-screen: 'Well Stan and I would be swimming along, we'd see a boat coming our way, we'd go like that [thumbing gesture again] and they would pick us up, wouldn't they Stanley?' As Ollie completes his bit, he leans back on the sofa, opens a book with customary, short-term self-satisfaction, and brings one leg up to lie on the upper part of his other leg (as if half-crossed). At the exact moment he moves into this posture, Stan leans across him, more prominently positioning himself towards Ollie's wife, and rests his elbow on Ollie's knee: as Ollie is bringing his leg up, Stan is already advancing to use it as a comfortable point of rest. A split-second too late and Stan might have recognised Ollie's recline, and his own shift might have appeared more calculated: Stan taking advantage of Ollie, albeit affectionately, as a prop. Moving in tandem, their synchronicity appears fond and touching. At the same time, Stan's nimble sense of direction, in relation to Ollie, is contrary to his nonsensical line about the direction of the boat: 'Of course that is if they were going our way mind you!'

Different objects (a music box, a sofa), other people (wives, policemen) and locations (steps, living rooms) are used to adjust the two performers' proximity and hence vary their dynamic and rhythm. The shot of Stan and Ollie is broken (now the two-shot is of Ollie and his wife) and so Ollie must enact a series of gestures, which although admirably self-styled fail to guarantee his self-assurance or, more significantly, his self-reliance. She asks, 'Are you telling me the truth?' Ollie replies indignantly, 'Do you think that a story like that could come from my mind, if it wasn't the truth?' As he says, 'mind', his hand, in the shape of a claw, touches his forehead, and as he says 'truth', this hand moves to touch his chest. Finally, he gives a disbelieving grunt, and adjusts her neck-scarf, raising it slightly, while fussily pretending to smarten (the neck-tie is straightened out rather than the explanation). The gestures have a declamatory air, and a grand progression (head, heart, wife), but each depends on the light touch of his fingertips, and once again, this aspect of finesse, while inflating the affectation (and the condescension), also pricks the

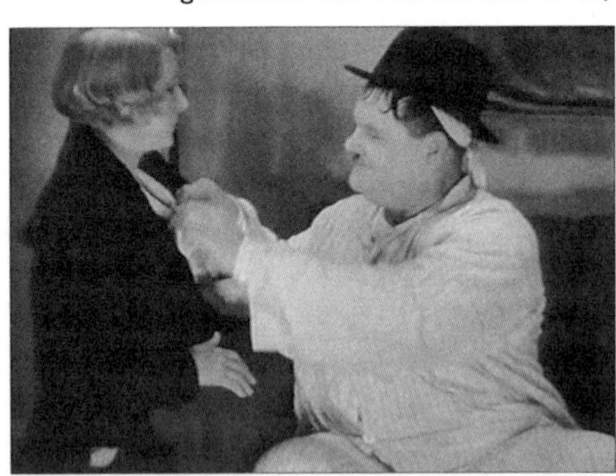

grandiose with the gentle. Ollie says, 'Why it's ridiculous. It's absurd' ('It's the silliest thing I ever heard', continues Stan creating a rhyme) as he gets up and cockily struts in front of the sofa, 'Why it is too far-fetched not to be the truth' (Stan thinks it 'impostrous', unlike his choice of vocabulary). As Ollie says 'truth', he raises his bowler and this appropriately reveals an incongruous nightcap. Ollie is unaware of what he has uncovered, and he twiddles the bowler as if to celebrate his confidence in the suitably 'farfetched' nature of revelation. Stan and Ollie are no longer permitted the comfort of a two-shot, so when Stan's wife asks, 'Is Oliver telling the truth?', he must now look across the room for Ollie's help. The film cuts to Ollie ('Go ahead and tell her'), who puts two fingers to his mouth, removes them and blows. The gesture is intended to remind Stan that should he cave in, Ollie will disclose his secret smoking forbidden by his wife. Yet, the gesture also appears to be Ollie blowing Stan a kiss, across the edit that now divides them, a reminder to Stan about genuine bonds of love and loyalty.

With this distance between them, Stan naturally confesses, and cries hysterically. The film cuts back to a (waist up) shot of Ollie who is now sitting at the table, with his head leaning on his arm; he looks in the direction of the camera. There is no attempt to shut Stan up, no attempt to excuse Stan's confession, no attempt to prolong the cover-up, no equal show of panic and after all their combined efforts at gesturing, Ollie now sits still, and separate. There is humour in the suddenness of his restraint. He looks towards us, now that he can no longer look to Stan, with the hope that we, at least (all of us, some of us, one of us), might recognise that his partner has let him down. His look is made more potent by the fact that he stares, not merely elsewhere,

but as if into another world, out of his own (fictional) world, the one that includes Stan. We might sympathise with the collapse into resignation and exhaustion, but we cannot confirm Ollie in his superiority, and not simply because, as is often claimed, he is in no position to condescend. We cannot take the side of one against the other, or accept that one of them is more at fault, or even, in each instance, start apportioning bits of blame. The reason for this is not sentiment, or magnanimity. Stan and Ollie are set up as apparently distinct entities, a view purported by publicity material (and perpetuated by lazy encyclopedia summaries): Stan is the thin one, Ollie the fat one; Stan is like a child to Ollie's pompous parent and so on. In fact, their behavioral and attitudinal characteristics continuously overlap, and this is enabled by their ever more involved and interdependent physical interactions.

Ollie does not talk to the camera in the manner of Groucho Marx: this would presume too much confidence, and permit a communication with the audience that was blunt and unambiguous. The effect is one of incompleteness; it differs from the smart performer sealing a moment by addressing a sneaky word in our direction, indulging the audience with a clever aside. The film uses Ollie's look to take mature advantage of the camera's status and of the possibilities offered by its ontology – an instrument that is always ambivalently straddling their world and ours – to present the problems of forming new unions. Ollie is permitted to address us, but it cannot bring him into our world (just as we cannot be brought into his). The camera is not even able, necessarily, to give him a view of us, although it does indeed present us with another view of him. The view presented is one of Ollie alone in the frame, stuck, unable to overcome the physical separation between performer and viewer. He must resume contact with his companion, despite their continual failings. Only then will he receive unfailing confirmation – 'didn't we Stanley?'

Suggesting perspectives: The Awful Truth

One of the finest sequences in Hollywood comedy for managing the distance between two people is the final scene of *The Awful Truth* (Leo McCarey, 1937). Jerry (Cary Grant) and Lucy Warriner (Irene Dunne) find themselves in adjacent bedrooms in Aunt Patsy's house in the country, divided by a faulty door, approximately one hour before midnight, at which time their divorce becomes official. The urgency of the deadline is set against their necessary tentativeness with each other: their agreement to avoid their divorce must be carefully managed so that they come together on the right terms. Neither of them will baldly state the terms of reconciliation, and their avoidance of saying exactly what they mean is not merely a consequence of stubbornness or self-deception – simply something to get over. Although there is inevitably more than a hint of inhibition in the precarious situation, their indirectness is necessary for them to move towards each other.

The scene plays with their separateness as a way of negotiating their reunion. Lucy sits down upon her bed after shooing away a black cat; as she sits, the door in front of her smoothly opens, as if it were triggered by her depression of the bed. The scene is shot from the far side of Lucy's bed, and since she has already turned off the light, she sits in darkness. As the door opens, Jerry is revealed before her in his large nightshirt, and suddenly put on a stage, framed by the doorframe and by the theatrical lighting (dark in the near bedroom, and lighter in his, the far bedroom). Jerry must sense this as a moment of revelation and sense the need to perform for her (in fresh ways), and so he balances on one leg and raises the other one, as if he might be lifted from the ground (in the oversized nightshirt and in the draughty country house). The gesture, appropriately one of precarious suspension, is checked by Grant to remain minimal: one leg remains carefully fixed to the floor, maintaining his position within the doorframe, and the movement of his arms and leg are unhurried. His act admits to his silly appearance, but coyly, and the constraint of the floating motion is a declaration of lightness (to her). This suggestiveness will now characterise their communication.

This flavour of communication prompts Lucy to say of the faulty door: 'not so very practical but I guess it will serve its purpose'. What does she take to be the purpose of the door's practical failure: will the door work adequately enough to keep them separate or will it be faulty enough to keep bringing them together? Her words fall gently and quietly, to almost a murmur, and this undemonstrative address gives room for the ambiguity to breathe. Indeed, Irene Dunne's voice *is* breathy, and slightly creaky, as if it were being gently stretched by the wind (her voice quietly quivering in the draught, perhaps, which drifts through the bedrooms on this windy night). It makes her sound dreamily far away – nearly lost yet lulling. A little later, when Lucy says 'goodnight', as she reclines, one simple and common pleasantry is made to sound complicated and uncommonly provocative. It is conclusive, curt – surely, you must curtail this exchange? It is sexually alluring, tantalising – surely, you are not prepared to curtail this exchange? It is a touch shaky, hesitant – surely, I should curtail this exchange? Lucy encourages, but furtively, by means of cautious rejection.

As in this single instance, so as the scene progresses, Lucy adopts the same pleasantry many times for a variety of purpose. Earlier, she says 'night' in shortened form, and is more straightforwardly impatient, while on the last occasion, upsetting Jerry's presumption that his place in her bed is assured she is gleeful, naughty, mocking.[5] Lucy's repeated use of 'goodnight' works in the same way as 'same' and 'different' in their ongoing conversation:

Lucy: Well, I mean if you didn't feel the way you feel, things wouldn't be the way they are, would they?
Jerry: But things are the way you made them.
Lucy: Oh no. They're the way you think I made them. I didn't make them that way at all. Things are just the same as they always were, only you're just the same, too, so I guess things will never be the same again.
And a little later...
Jerry: You're wrong about things being different because they are not the same. Things are different, except in a different way. You're still the same, only I've been a fool. Well, I'm not now. So, as long as I'm different, don't you think things could be the same again? Only a little different.

The repeat of identical words ('goodnight', 'same', 'different'), each time variously moulded, sustains the tenor of suggestiveness (Dunne conducts her vocal variations exquisitely with flitting eyelids and floating eyebrows). It also gives coherence and consistency to the style of the performances (and the sequence). The use of 'same' and 'different' is necessary for the characters' covert negotiation, but it is also an analogy for their style of performance: different inflections are given to the same words rather than delivering distinctly different words.

The same words may be appreciated from different perspectives. By merely saying 'goodnight', Lucy invites Jerry to appreciate her differently: she excites his interest through complicating herself, and arouses varied prospects. Appropriately, the film never views Lucy, or her room, from the perspective of Jerry's room, perhaps because Jerry, for most of the scene, refuses to view Lucy appropriately. Instead, we frequently watch Jerry from the perspective of Lucy's room, and there is the sense of Jerry having to come to (understand) Lucy (while she waits for him on her bed). After the first ellipse, they are shown separately, both lying awake in bed, followed by a close-up of the door handle shuddering. When the film cuts to a medium shot, however, the perspective is crucially from Lucy's room. It is from this location that we experience the opening of the door. As it opens, Lucy lies in bed in the foreground, and Jerry is shown through the doorframe, also lying in bed, in the background. On realising their exposure to each other, they simultaneously raise their upper bodies to sit up in their separate beds. There is a considerable pause after the door opens; they are caught short, before they proudly enact their defensive rise, and sit to attention, on guard. The performers' shift in posture, in relation to the door and camera, crisply encapsulates the scene's concerns. The seemingly supernatural opening of the door enables us to see them move in time together, while separated, and with Jerry *farthest away*. (The door cannot resolve their problems; its smooth glide is suitably aloof from the quick agitation of their rise.)

In one moment early in the scene, Lucy stands close against the wall immediately next to the door. We only see her alone in this position for a few seconds because Jerry's opening of the door soon interrupts, and this ensures that the motivations for her movement remain elusive. It appears, at first, that she is merely snatching an opportunity to listen into his room, but any such opportunism quickly bleeds into something more indefinite. Is she allowing herself a move towards him, while safely maintaining their separation? Is she willing the door to open during a precious period of its closure? The glimpse means we have only suggestions of Lucy's private equivocations, but it deepens the scrutiny of suggestiveness by hinting at the personal uncertainty lurking behind her efforts at controlling ambiguity.

Lucy's private gestures of anxiety are complex and ambivalent, but Jerry's anxiety pushes his private gestures to the point of caricature. We see him lying on his bed, staring off-screen right towards the window, with his head resting on his fist. He suddenly raises his head with a jerk, and then looks off-screen left towards the door. There is then a pan to the window, whereupon Jerry enters the shot and raises the frame. After letting the wind gust into the room, he stands upright with his arms in front of him, his hands joined together at his waist. The film then follows the gust and pans towards the door, which stubbornly refuses to open. It then cuts back to him, with an expression of disbelief, and with his hands now on his hips. From Lucy's room the black cat is holding the door with front leg and paw outstretched, and the deliberate determination of its posture seems to reflect human motivation, or the anthropomorphic behaviour of an animated cat. The cat's action is incredible, taken alone, but Jerry's gestures also take on a cartoon aspect (the cat is Tom, perhaps, to Grant's Jerry). His over-accentuated jerk of the head resembles a character from a cartoon from Fred Quimby or Tex Avery, one who has just had another good idea, with the memory of all recently-failed schemes wiped away. His upright stance, as he waits for the successful completion to his plan, has an air of blind self-satisfaction; and his hands on his hips exclaim an exaggerated disappointment. Jerry's cartoon postures do not seem animated, however; rather they are individually proclaimed as though a figure in a comic strip: unequivocal postures, clearly drawn, each one combining the emphatic with the static.

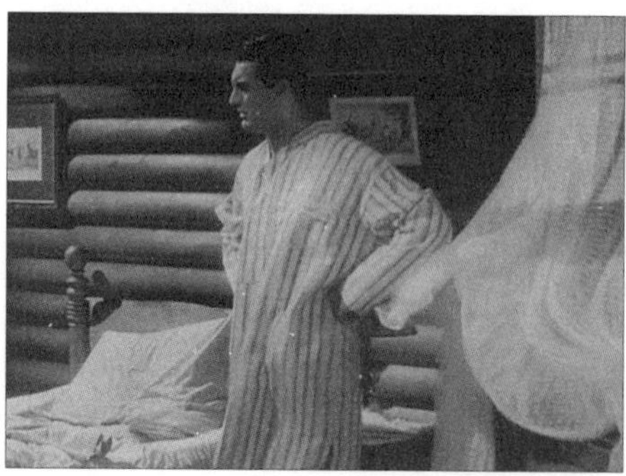

Grant's gestures for Jerry are deliberately over-demonstrative because he is anxiously demonstrating to himself. Without Lucy to move him, he only has himself to entertain. In comparison to those he adopts in the company of Lucy, his gestures are artificial and indelicate, and they fail to suggest the possibility and promise that will sustain interest in his personality. He behaves like a child self-consciously immersed in playing games, rather than accepting his adult responsibility to share his child-like capacity to be playful.[6] As the cat moves away and the door opens, he is now crawling on all fours. The film continues to maintain the view from Lucy's room so that we see Jerry as Lucy sees him: suspended in the doorway, immobilised, incapable of a confident entry. His shifty attempts at approaching her reflect how slowly he shifts his perspective of her.

However, during his moment of genuine repentance, in front of Lucy, he smoothly runs together a series of gestures, and they show Grant's irresistibly charming ability to erase complication with ease of movement. He stands, hands behind his back, nervously swaying, and she says 'No more being...' His interruption then consists of bringing his arms from behind his back, folding them in front of his chest, rotating his left arm like the hand of a clock across his face to reveal a big grin, and then finally resting the hand of the same arm at his chin. Initially, with his arms behind his back he looks in a meek position, finally accepting of her verdict. Crossing his arms appears to be a defensive move, but one arm quickly rotates, interrupts her, seems to say, 'You need say no more', and admits guilt. Yet, it also disallows Lucy from speaking any specific points of discontent (and allows him not to speak of any specific misdemeanours). The rotating arm is full of the joy of simple mime: it wipes the slate clean; his sunny face emerges from behind a cloud. Only a slight lowering of his arm allows his hand to move to his chin, and for him to look confused. 'There's only one thing that bothers me', he says, but as Lucy sternly replies, 'What?' the door bangs into him from behind. It reminds him to stop remembering, while nudging him back towards the suggestive once again (and back towards Lucy's bed).

Lucy glances at a chair and then her eyes drift back towards the bed: Jerry finally receives the signal from Lucy that will grant him permission to re-enter her domain. Jerry jams the chair back under the door handle and then stands upright like a young boy at a school awards ceremony, next in line, waiting to be called, and straining to adopt the correct posture. Excited by the sudden attention and eager to receive the inevitable prize, he also sports a cheeky grin that undermines the propriety. Lucy clutches her blanket tightly up to her chin, says 'goodnight', and begins a mocking giggle. The shot of the clock which closes the film, shows, on the stroke of their official separation, the male figure following the female figure into her hole. This would seem suggestive enough to be conclusive. Yet, the penultimate view is indeterminate: when Jerry should be, at least, moving to bring them together, Lucy's giggling off-screen suspends him once again. He stands separated (like Charlie and Ollie before him?) – bereft and bemused.

Staging perspectives: The Philadelphia Story

The Philadelphia Story (George Cukor, 1940) sees Cary Grant again positioned on the edge of things. He plays C. K. Dexter Haven – former husband to Tracy Lord (Katherine Hepburn) and now hoping to win her back. Unfortunately, Tracy is to marry George Kitteridge (John Howard) but plans have been upset because Tracy has spent the eve of her wedding frolicking with Macaulay 'Mike' Connor (James Stewart). He is a journalist who is reluctantly reporting on her high-society wedding along with photographer Elizabeth 'Liz' Imbrie (Ruth Hussey) who is in love with him.

On the morning of the wedding, Dinah (Virginia Weidler), Tracy's young sister, is talking to Uncle Willie (Roland Young) on the large patio area in front of the house; she says of her much older sister Tracy: 'If she marries anyone, it's just got to be Mr. Connor.' On this line, the film cuts to Dexter entering between the columns surrounding the patio, from off-screen right, *making an entrance* into an already established stage area. His entrance is smoothly related to his cue line as he immediately responds to Dinah: 'Why Dinah, what makes you think she should?' We have the sense of him 'waiting in the wings' and the film quite deliberately makes use of the stage convention. The sense of 'wings', however, is transformed by the different ontology of film, where the world continues beyond the confines of the frame. The 'wings' can be conceived as a distinct place in the world of the film – by the area of the swimming pool, perhaps, which we know to exist just behind the patio area – and we are teased with the possibility that he has been waiting nearby, just out of shot. Has he been sitting a little out of their reach, strategically waiting for his moment? We are denied an establishing perspective of his entrance that might clarify the details of his approach. His entrance, timed to perfection, and which would be conventional, even essential, on a stage, seems contrived on film. By such a contrivance, however, the film hints that there was no approach to show, and that the suddenness of his appearance is magical.

Indeed, Dexter may be a celestial presence hovering on the edge of things, interfering vividly and yet influencing indirectly. He floats free of traditional dress with an airy, light-coloured jacket without the traditional lapels: casual, but it cuts smart and sharp (while the large-*winged* collar of his shirt flaps over his suit). Does he shape events or wait for them to take their course? (A few seconds before his final departure George says to Dexter, 'I have a feeling you had something to do with all this', to which Dexter replies, 'Possibly but you were a great help.') His involvement in, and power over, the development and outcome of events remains mysterious. When Tracy enters the scene with her hangover, she sits on the couch, and Dexter perches himself to her left, on the arm of the couch, neither quite on it, nor completely off. (Dinah stands behind the couch, on her right shoulder, hovering like a fiendish imp, mischievously poking at Tracy with her words. In fact, Tracy addresses her as a 'little fiend' just a minute later, and she could well be Dexter's helpful sprite, Ariel to his Prospero. Dexter, a few moments later, gives her instruction: 'If the conversation should lag, you might tell Tracy about your dream.')[7] The performers are often positioned, as they are here, quite front on to the camera. They avert their look, and do not directly address each other as they speak their lines. Once again, there is

a proscenium effect, with the performers 'obeying' basic stage decorum, as if they needed simultaneously to 'speak out' to a live audience in an auditorium. The indirect content and tenor of the dialogue is enhanced by this manner of positioning.

The film exploits simple conventions of stage positioning to explore aspects of avoidance and evasion (what is conventional on stage becomes significant on film). When the characters are close to each other, they tend to sit or stand side by side: on the couch, Tracy and Dexter do turn toward each other, but cannot face each other for long. Their natural inclination, because of the pull of their posture, is to turn back, towards the front. Dexter's evasions are because he must wait for others; he is not yet *in a position* to 'behave naturally' (only supernaturally). He remains at the periphery, even though he eagerly wishes to return to the centre of the group – or eye to eye with Tracy. Cary Grant has the distinction *to stand apart*, making him appear pointed and poised, purposeful and passive. A few moments later Dexter brings Tracy a hangover cure and they sit facing each other: the film offers a glimpse of them differently situated. Tracy soon pulls away, however, and after a phone call to George, sits on a chair,

at the dining table, and faces away from Dexter. She is low in the frame. Dexter approaches, but halts at a position behind her and to the left, and leans on the back of the adjacent chair. 'I'm such an unholy mess of a girl', she moans, and Dexter replies, 'Well that's no good, that's not even conversation.' If the resumption and continuation of conversation is crucial for the couple learning to come together again (as it is in *The Awful Truth*), then the failure to converse is here expressed through a difficulty in finding, or maintaining, positions that would allow them to continue a conversation.[8]

Tracy reaches out behind her to find the touch of his hand. Given her posture, this is an uncomfortable gesture for Hepburn to enact, but it is precisely expressive of Tracy trying to reach towards awkward places, and of her now realising what she must grasp. Following their touch of hands, he moves to sit next to her, making their positions more equable. Her effort has prompted Dexter to move to her level, and allowed them both to *feel* a human being again. Previously ethereal, for a moment at least, her human touch has released them: Tracy no longer a goddess, Dexter no longer celestial. ('And do you know how I feel?' she says to her father in the final minutes of the film. For her father she is, at last, what others have taken her to be before her redemption: 'Like a queen, like a goddess.' But she happily replies that she feels 'Like a human, like a human being.') Dexter says, 'Tell me, what did you think of my wedding present?' and by referring to the model of their yacht 'True Love' he is able to summon romantic apparitions of their past. Tracy says that 'she was *yar* alright' but 'I wasn't was I?' (a reference to the 'True love' whose wonder on the seas can only be described as '*yar*'). As Dexter replies, 'Not very', he pulls up his knees to the height of his chest and his feet onto the chair, an eccentric position when contrasted to the correct seating of high society. (It is a position he adopts on a few occasions in the film: after socking Mike, for example, when they sit, side by side, on the ground.) Comfortable as this position may be for him, he seems to be wrapping himself up, or gathering himself up, in this moment of unease. Could this be the favoured seating position of a goblin or a pixie? Possibly, but continuing his enquiry about his wedding gift, he announces that 'I like my presents to be at least acknowledged', where 'presents' sounds like 'presence' – 'I like my presence to be acknowledged' – and where Dexter wittily challenges his existence as supernatural.

Grant finds perched positions from where Dexter can effectively pun. The group is gathered together, and as George enters, he moves to the end of the line. He takes his place on a chair that faces off-screen right, but his side is against its back (rather than his back against its back), and so he is side on to the rest of the group. He is strategically hinged: he can direct his head towards the group, speak out in front of him, or turn his upper body away. His is able to shift with agility, and in a position to adjust meanings; able to twist himself flexibly, he may turn

words around (Mike says, 'doubtless you remember', and Dexter interjects, 'doubtless, without a doubt.' George says 'A man expects his wife...' and Tracy interrupts, 'to behave herself – naturally [i.e. as one would expect]' which allows Dexter's interjection, 'To behave herself *naturally* [i.e. true to her nature].') Each time he interjects, the film cuts to show him alone in closer shot, and these cuts have the jarring effect of emphasising his moments of involvement, while cutting him off from the group. Indeed, the characters are all lined up as if on a stage, but again the 'staginess' successfully appears as standing (or sitting) uncomfortably – suspended. The performers make use of 'staginess' as a way of presenting characters whose presentation of themselves is effortful, or artificial.

Meanwhile, the film cuts them into smaller groups that seem incomplete, and keeps the situation inconclusive. Mike, for example, leaves Liz alone on the left, to move across right, into a sub-grouping with Tracy and George. On the stage, characters can move into various sub-groupings, but on film, the camera can also frame them, and make us particularly conscious of exclusions, those who are feeling left out of the picture (like Dexter, or Liz). This technique is especially potent when those excluded are adjacent: they are so close to, and yet just held off from, their best arrangement.

The rigidity of theatrical blocking is deliberately courted to create a stiffness that in turn can be released. With George expunged ('you're on the way out, the lot of you!' he announces, at the moment he departs alone), and on hearing the wedding music coming from the house, the characters move anxiously into the interior lounge area. Everyone is gathered for the wedding but there is no groom. The Tracy/Dexter/Mike/Liz situation is now satisfyingly worked out, without looking as if it is being ponderously worked through. The film avoids presenting negotiations in series, and appearing too careful. The execution is masterly, arriving at situations that seem destined, after entertaining alternatives that seem credible. The film makes Mike's proposal serious and passionate, and inappropriate. It presents him as dedicated to his proposal, and very properly convinced by the rejection. James Stewart scrutinises his propensity to perform sincerity: Mike's proposal is heartfelt despite his realisation that it may be mistaken. Tracy's rejection is also shown to be sensible although an alternative decision remained an option, and was not ridiculous. The situation is tightly held together without being cosy, and the economy of expression is justified as tactful.

The rapid adjustments between the couples seem apposite, the consequence of an inspiring lucidity after extended periods of avoidance. Tracy and Mike stand facing each other in a medium close two-shot. Mike says, 'Will you marry me Tracy?' For three seconds we watch Tracy, her head still, and her mouth quivering. Then the film cuts to show Dexter standing stiffly behind Tracy, flat up against the wall, with a look of gravity. He is still at the edge but seems held back rather than holding back, gripped, and it is clear that despite the cutaway, of two seconds, he is no longer in that pivotal position to pun. It is a shot that deepens our experience of Dexter, because it confirms that his control

is not total, his place at the periphery is not necessarily temporary, and he has not been smugly hanging around for the inevitable. The film then makes the first of a series of cuts to Liz, also seperated, waiting. It then returns to Tracy: 'Thanks, but no', she says, 'I don't think Liz would like it, I am not sure you would, and I'm even a little doubtful about myself.' There is a second cutaway to Dexter as she says 'myself', partly because this line lets Dexter back in. This return to Dexter is also triggered by 'a little doubtful', because it shows she now conceives of herself with doubt, and it is the acknowledgement of self-doubt – which Dexter has been advocating as a quality – that will give her the strength to return to him. Despite the cut to Dexter, Tracy does not stop speaking after 'myself', and after a very short intake of breath, she immediately continues with an inspiring appreciation of Mike: 'but I am beholden to you, Mike, I am *most* beholden.' As we hear the first 'I am...' we are still looking at Dexter, and the cut back to Tracy is on the first 'beholden.' The word 'beholden' is already striking: Hepburn's stirring delivery of an archaic past participle is uncannily attuned to the present moment. Yet, the emotional effect of 'beholden' is further enhanced by the emphasis of the edit because the earlier cut to Dexter allowed the possibility of a return to Tracy at this crucial juncture. Her line of refusal is already resonantly benevolent, but the film's generosity is heightened further because the shot that re-establishes Tracy's bond to Dexter in turn intensifies how 'beholden' she is to Mike.

The editing has re-established the bond between Tracy and Dexter, but physical confirmation will require that they overcome some more awkward angles. Tracy stands at the doorway through which the congregation waits for the ceremony to begin, and she interrupts the music. The crowd all turn to look over their shoulders, while, on the other side of the door, Dexter awaits on Tracy's shoulder, back to the wall, holding her wedding hat, and hidden from the sight of guests. Caught at this transitional point, Tracy says, 'Dexter, Dexter. What next?' He replies, 'Two years ago, I did you out of wedding in this house, by eloping to Maryland...' and she repeats the lines to the congregation, 'Two years ago...' At this moment, Dexter moves swiftly to his right; he takes the ring off mother, hands the hat to father, and gives the ring to Mike (who is 'honoured' to be his best man). Dexter falls back into place just as Tracy, having finished repeating his words, is faltering and he says, 'which was very bad manners'. In only a few seconds – in a similar spirit to the edit on 'beholden' – Dexter helps Tracy, unites the rest of the ensemble (mother, father, Mike and Liz), and returns to her rescue, just in time. Dexter continues, 'but I hope to make it up to you by going through with it now – as originally planned.' Tracy continues to repeat and Hepburn combines a series of compelling vocal modulations with physical convulsions.

Hepburn's performance, all deliberations and exaggerations of voice and posture, is perfectly suited to Tracy's demonstrating and role-playing. Stressed words or positions also allow, in turn, the relaxation of her voice and body. Wishing to urgently continue her repetition, she speaks hurriedly, 'but I hope to make it up to you by...' As she says 'by', her left hand and arm, which was tensely outstretched, and pushed up against the doorframe, is released and drifts free, like a pianist's hands leaving, and then hovering above, the keys at the end of a piece. Tracy then turns to look at Dexter, and her arm trembles, nearly touching him on his chest (as if to stroke him), but instead springs back, and, as she turns again to face the throng, it drops, relieved, behind her back, where Dexter finally takes hold of it. This gesture of ecstatic hesitation takes place as she stutters on 'by', and then continues, '...by going *beautifully* through with it, as was originally and most *beautifully* planned.' She looks one way, but is pulled another, and this is caught in her voice: deliberate, stated and stately, relishing the performance of a grand announcement, and punctured, 'beautifully', by a high pitched vibrato wobble.

Finally, they embrace each other, and confirm, and celebrate, each other's risks and doubts. Tracy says, 'Are you sure?' and Dexter says, 'Not in the least'; Tracy says, 'I'll be *yar* now – I promise to be *yar*') and Dexter says, 'Be whatever you like, you're my redhead.' This line provides confirmation, if it were needed, that in turning towards Dexter, she has learned to behave, not as one should be ('to behave – naturally'), but as one could be ('to behave naturally'). As they now look directly at each other, she sees that he is able to see her, and understands that they are able to see each other. No wonder that they clutch so tightly. They do not simply hold each other, at last, but they take a hold of

each other, hold each other in this position, face to face. The film shows it to be a beautiful position, and all the more so for being easily disturbed. The shot at the close of the film, which freezes Dexter, Tracy and Mike as their picture is taken, shows them shocked and surprised. Once again they are looking out, elsewhere, away from each other; they are awkwardly turned, and side by side.

Without impressing us with manoeuvres, all the sequences in this chapter are especially attentive to the performers' positions in relation to each other; developing, and deepening, arrangements. Equally, the performers and the camera are mutually, and quietly, respectful, neither upstaging the other. The camera, for example, rarely performs any pronounced demonstrations of its own. Their relationship is intimate and involved, but uncomplicated. And together, the performers and the camera, confidently positioned, appropriately aligned, create a vivid sense of place...

2 PLACE

A place to change: The Scarlet Empress

An appreciation of the effectiveness of performance in *The Scarlet Empress* (Josef von Sternberg, 1934), especially that of Marlene Dietrich, depends acutely on understanding its synthesis with location. In a pivotal sequence in the film the young Catherine the Great, formerly called Sophia (Dietrich), is helping The Empress (Louise Dresser) who rules Russia on behalf of idiot Peter (Sam Jaffe), prepare for bed. The Empress has been engaged in a long running affair with the Count Alexei (John Lodge) and now, having heard that Catherine has become involved with him, intends to humiliate her. The Empress says, 'I wouldn't advise you to become my rival', and young Catherine replies 'Rival? What does Your Majesty mean?' The four minutes of screen time that follow dramatise Catherine's transformation from a flirtatious girl frolicking on the cusp of womanhood to the hardened Catherine the Great.

The performances that surround Dietrich are vivid, but not alive; they are fantastic pieces of furniture. The Old Empress is presented as a piece of the ancient architecture of the palace – around which the youthful Catherine has scampered – closely related to the grotesque gargoyles which fill the palace and now surround the pair in the bedroom. Both women sit on the large four-poster bed and the film alternates between close-ups of them. The Empress acts as a mirror to Catherine's features, distorting but prescient. Both have ringlets of hair dropping down by the side of their face, but where Catherine's ringlets bounce, each of them fluffed up and teased out (and crowned by an adornment of fruit and flowers), The Empress' are unyielding, hard set and crusty, like a horsehair wig. The large 'V' of Catherine's dress, which rises from her cleavage to the corner of her shoulders, is fresh animal fur and on Catherine still running wild. Against this, the ermine 'V' that adorns The Empress' gown seems artificial and worn by occasion. The strong back lighting refines Catherine's features: her ringlets, glowing at their edge, are magically formed from springy golden wisps; her glossed dark lips, shaped and lined into a compact rose bud with taut upper bow, are shiny and moist, dew kissed; and her face, free from glare, is soft and smooth, her cheeks allowed to show their delicate rouge. The Empress is unflatteringly lit, darkness lodging in the cracks of her aged face, creating crevices. Catherine is made-up to show the surface signs of the blood that courses within her, but her matt complexion, lightly powdered and slightly dry, suggests the possibility of the grey stone of the Empress' countenance.

The Empress asks Catherine to blow out all the candles, only at ease perhaps when her features blend completely with the dark stone surrounds and her own crevices are hidden. Catherine sits, wide-eyed, on the verge of being mesmerised, and then, her stare remaining fixed on the Empress, her face darkens, and she slips away. (Because the movements of her lower body are excluded, she appears to mechanically slide off-screen.) The background of the shot now comes into focus and consists of a gargoyle head and an accompanying candle; three seconds later, she re-emerges at the back of the frame. Her profile pokes into the left-hand corner of the same frame from which she had just disappeared and her hand touches the lower portion of the gargoyle's chin. She is tiny both in relation to the preceding close-up (of

her) and to the expansive gargoyle and candle that now fill the bulk of the frame. Despite her tiny appearance, her presence casts a shadow over the gargoyle, distorting the clarity of its outline, and so as she quietly blows out the candle, her blow appears to be an affectionate bedtime kiss upon its forehead. Her profile then disappears from the screen, but there is a slight delay before her hand pulls away: she detaches herself discreetly, but fondly, from a child she has just lulled to sleep.

This begins a series of shots where Dietrich is placed in compositional harmony with gargoyles and candles. She takes up these positions during a mysterious soundtrack that seems the consequence of a spell cast by the Empress. 'Before you retire you can be of one more service', she says and then, as she turns her head and upper body to the right, she is suddenly shrouded in dark shadow. Similarly, a monotonous chiming begins, as if from nowhere. Presumably, another candle has been extinguished, and a clock has struck the hour, but the very turn of her head seems to have altered the light and sound. She then announces, 'Behind my mirror a concealed passage will lead you down a flight of stairs to another door.' As she begins, on the word 'Behind', the film cuts immediately to another shot of a gargoyle. Dislocated from the performer in space and by tone, the voice seems celestial: no longer harsh and hectoring, her delivery is soft and beguiling. Her words do not simply instruct therefore, they hypnotise, and Catherine, as if in a trance – gladly obedient, calmly possessed – sneaks snugly into position between candle and gargoyle. She does this on three occasions, and each time she enters and exits a still frame. On entering, there is a sense of sidling in from behind and completing the décor, a crucial missing piece at last restored; on departing, she slopes off behind the statue, and her hand lags behind, reluctant to let go, caressing the gargoyle as it is finally dragged free. Her soft hand strokes the rough, hard, cold stone as if she were bringing the inanimate inhabitants of the palace to life by erotic stimulation. Yet, on each touch, while she seduces into devotion, they suck the blood out of her (so that she will be like them, hardened and cold). Her face, more dullish white now, blends with stone, her lacquered lips *set* like the gargoyle's hard moustache. In each frame, she mirrors the gargoyle's appearance and expression: versions, inversions, of each other.

The film now locates the sound of the chimes – which provided the hypnotic background support to the Empress' words – by cutting to a close-up of a clock (withheld until this moment to suggest a supernatural origin). Violent little figurines, holding medieval weaponry and instruments of torture, move around, and around, in and out of the dark hole below the clock face. The Empress' turn of the head initiated a series of turns in the sequence, and the figurines now rhyme with Catherine's moves around the gargoyles as she gradually turns into a different version of herself. Time passes but terrifying figures will keep coming around. As a secret back door is opened, Catherine turns and then turns again to close it, and her rotation within the frame of the doorway is steady and fluent, mechanical like the clock, whose chimes accompany her. She appears like a pirouetting doll in a music box, and as the door silently closes, the chimes cease. Because she is in full silhouette, her outline is accentuated, emphasising the doll shape, while at the same time she is black – not white and clean – a photographic inversion of the familiar revolving figure. During this moment, most of the expressive details available to Dietrich as a performer – nuances of face, voice and gesture – are absent but her presence, carefully shaped by her integration in the surrounding environment, is eloquent.

The integration of performer and environment effectively express changes in scale; Dietrich's body and costume are placed in relation to the surrounds to adjust her shape and size. Catherine seems squashed into the small stairway as she descends, still looking like a girl – rather like Alice after a potion, too big for the tiny doors and passageways of Wonderland – but one now growing to fill her surroundings. Her proximity to the walls is emphasised by her raised left arm, her palm patting the surface as she clip-clops down the steps. Her increasing intimacy with the décor, throughout the sequence, is intimately connected

to her touching it; the tactility is potent, and here the image of Dietrich's hand and the sound of her feet draw out the textures. On hearing Catherine, Count Alexei quickly swivels away; she comes through a large thick, heavy door and while she faces off-screen right, he vanishes behind her back to ascend the stairs. On hearing movement she performs another slow turn, curious and apprehensive, and the slowness of the turn is enhanced by her width: her bulbous crinoline skirt, her puffed sleeves and the thick fur 'V' pushing up and spreading out her chest and shoulders. She moves her arm to the doorframe perhaps to steady her while she trembles. Her fingers stroke a triangular gash in the frame and as she turns to see, and apprehend – her half-open mouth rhymes with the gash, frozen in realisation and anticipation – she touches sensuously (a gentle fingering of the hard surface). Her sexual initiation is separate from an actual sexual engagement, and corresponds to the Empress' execution, and manipulation, of power. Catherine is left to her own touch, while forced into thinking of the illicit sex of others. Her expression of inwardness is provocatively sexualised by suppression and furtiveness.

The crowning shot of the sequence soon follows, where Catherine matures before our eyes, transforming herself into the Scarlet Empress. The shot only lasts 15 seconds but it is economical and dense, one of the most richly achieved moments of transformation in cinema. It is a summation of the concerns of the sequence – shaping this soft woman and hardening her – and an occasion to view the performer in exquisite symbiosis with her environment. Performer and surrounds meld, and Dietrich is well *cast*. Catherine follows Count Alexei running up the stairs that she had only a moment ago descended. Her urgent ascent is viewed from the top of the stairs, and she gets ever closer, eventually enveloping the image: she runs headlong into a darkness that she herself creates. This is the point at which the film moves back inside the bedroom and the Count shuts the secret door. This grained wooden door fills the frame, and dissolves slightly, decreasing in prominence, to show Catherine standing behind. The wood is patterned with a 'V' shape, and the dissolve allows it to graphically match the 'V' of Catherine's dress, gluing the images together, and tightening the superimposition. She seems to occupy exactly the same space as the door; a ghostly figure caught walking through a wall. She stares out, as if watching them, and because we are able to see her, through the solid door, it appears that she is able to see through it. She does in fact *see* even though she cannot see (into the room). Indeed, the door then evaporates completely, and as Catherine is left clear in the image, she is left to see a clear picture. Suddenly, she sees through everything.

Dissolving its 'V' into her 'V', the door appears to melt into her (perhaps only to strengthen again once inside her). Catherine is lit so that dark patches become prominent under her eyebrows, nostrils, cheekbones and jaw line. Dietrich has pronounced features and they swallow areas of light, allowing for stark contrasts of colour across her face. The film now takes advantage of these possibilities offered by the performer's face: dark patches contrast with her stony white skin, hardening her features, no longer softly rounded. She is more strongly defined, angular, looking older, but also like a statue, seeming colder. Suddenly she looks like poster images of Dietrich, posed and stilled, iconic, like the icons of the palace. Her doughy, young skin always appeared malleable: gradually warmed, and then heated, by each of the candle flames, it is now finally baked. She is at first slightly crouched forward, as if peering, but then she straightens up and leans back, a slight movement in distance, but a large dramatic shift. As if receiving a serum, she is invaded, her control removed, but also becalmed, enjoying a tranquil pleasure. She closes her eyes, as if falling back into a deep sleep. She is nearly a corpse, but for her chest rising and falling. A little death, perhaps. Stretching back, tensing up, chest heaving, she invites all that is hard to enter her.

Throughout this climax, Catherine's movement and interaction with her environment is enhanced by the surrounding music, an expression both of the palace and her feelings, nourishing their symbiosis. The sudden burst of a hunting horn calls Catherine to hurry up the steps. As the Count opens the secret door there is a tremolo, a convention of suspense or hesitation, but here specifically associated with the door that will soon tremble and dissolve. A military theme occurs in brass and wind, accompanying the Count in uniform, and all that is formal, stern and without spontaneity within the bedroom. The strings provide a rhythm that matches Catherine's breathing – her heartbeat perhaps – and represent the last bursts of life on the other side of the door. When she finally descends the steps, both palms touch the walls, not only to steady, but also to provide support in another sense: she needs more than ever to be touched, on both sides, by the wall's cold surface. The strings also descend, and slow, despondent, but are answered by the militaristic wind and brass, rising and exhorting.

A place to hide: There's Always Tomorrow

The opening of *There's Always Tomorrow* (Douglas Sirk, 1956) has two consecutive sequences structured around the same domestic environment. A telephone rings and in the background of the shot, a young teenager (Ellen Groves; Gigi Perreau) eagerly runs down some stairs, passes a large front door at the base of the stairs, and then comes toward the foreground of the image. She lies down on the floor, on an imaginary line in the open plan between hallway and lounge. With telephone in hand, she talks about 'boys' to her friend, and her legs and feet casually kick up from the knee. At the same time the camera moves right and forwards to meet her, itself passing the chair and desk in the extreme foreground, at first showing her movement down and through the architecture of the house, and then joining her, close up, to point up the little patch in which she settles. While the camera attends to her movements within the home, the character pays little attention: indeed, precisely by taking her home for granted, she expresses a familiarity and comfort within it.

Her elder brother Vincent (William Reynolds) soon takes the telephone away from her so that he may speak to his fiancée. While talking on the telephone, he settles at the front left-hand side of the frame, and his father, Clifford Groves (Fred MacMurray), enters through the front door at the back of the shot. The son does not turn to wish his father 'Good Evening'; indeed, he barely acknowledges him. When Clifford shouts to his wife, his son finally turns and tells him to 'shhhh'. This begins a pattern in the sequence of Clifford left behind, left stranded in his house. This abandonment, however, is also shown as undramatic and unsurprising, a middle-aged father caught up in the familial run of things. MacMurray captures both these senses in his performance. He shows some annoyance, and wishes he could show some more – he is especially restrained considering he has been trying to reach his wife on the telephone for the previous couple of hours – but his attitude remains mild and patient. His physical placement establishes his situation, and so the performer need not openly acknowledge his *position*; he remains appropriately subdued, and maintains his mild-mannered persona, but the film does not subdue the significance of his exclusion.

Equally, the film is able to characterise the children's selfishness as youthful self-absorption, and frees them from performing a selfishness that may be too explicit or direct. They do seem precocious and conceited, but they are also shown to be 'typical kids', caught up in their own concerns, unconsciously finding or creating separate paths (around the house) from their parents. The youngest girl, Frankie (Judy Nugent), flies down the stairs, says a passing 'hello' to her father, and scurries around him into the kitchen. The film then cuts to a shot of the kitchen where the home help, Mrs Rogers (Jane Darwell), is ironing her sash. It seems to be from Clifford's viewpoint (in direction and distance), as he is left outside the kitchen to look in. 'Just suppose you stay and supervise', announces the home help, and she and the girl proceed to have a little comic exchange. Significantly, however, on the first word, 'Just', the film cuts back to Clifford going up the stairs, and like him we listen, rather than see, the exchange. The dialogue consists of only a few lines, it tells of nothing serious and neither home help nor his daughter are deliberately ignoring him, but the film establishes an undramatic exclusion suggesting that the sounds of domestic life are routinely heard from another place.

The camera calmly locates the characters' dynamics. As Clifford finally meets his wife, Marion (Joan Bennett), on the landing, we view from the lower portion of stairs, not too far away, but noticeably kept at a distance. The camera is like a guest, politely dropping back on a first visit, perhaps a little wary, nervously aware of some tension between the couple (Marion responds to his bunch of flowers with cool and perfunctory hyperbole: 'Oh, they're beautiful'). Their greetings take place on the upstairs landing, a transitional place, where the family meet and pass in transit between their private domains. He kisses her, but her posture remains stiff and upright, a touch impatient, and slightly indignant as if he had caught her off-guard in public, and they *are* in public in one sense: their few seconds together are soon broken by Ellen's run on to the landing. The camera, still at a distance – tactfully perhaps, but also reflecting the couple's lack of intimacy – calmly moves right, imperturbably, quite prepared to take in her careless, but inevitable, interruption. She cries 'Mother ... can I borrow?' and Marion replies, '*May* I borrow?' preferring to correct her grammar rather than her rudeness, and sure enough she runs straight past her father while shouting, 'Thank you Mum ... Hi Dad.' The camera finally moves to a more intimate position, whereupon Marion presents a safe cheek to be kissed, which he duly pecks, allowing her to rush off to find a place in the home for the flowers – 'I'll put them in a vase.' (The moment of giving and receiving flowers is often too quickly curtailed by the need to put them in water; the practical task prevents the couple from dwelling.)

The performers' placement within the home reveals latent aspects of character and situation that are kept in abeyance by other elements of their performance. Clifford insists on dealing with the flowers, enabling him to grasp some control (of his movement, and those around him) while disrupting her evasions (although he and Marion may only be dimly aware of these intentions). He moves into the en-suite washroom in their bedroom, which is in the foreground of the shot; it is thinly spread, like a walk-in wardrobe, and he prepares the flowers, while she hovers just outside, within the bedroom. Clifford is assertive and generous, taking control so others are freed from worrying: he announces that he has got Marion's birthday evening 'all arranged', tells her to 'go and get dolled up', and continues to set out the plans ('We'll drive into Los Angeles ... Cocktails ... Dinner at...'). Yet his movement in the space undermines his best endeavours: his desire for them to break out is rather at odds with his domestic task, and his confinement in this slither of a washroom. Despite his confidence in expanding on the direction their evening will take, the effect of being hemmed in, of having little room to manoeuvre, is accentuated by the fact that he is sharing this small space with the camera and Ellen to the right who is fiddling about in her mother's clothing drawers.

After hemming Clifford in, the film pulls the activity away into other locations, while he views from outside. Sometimes he cannot even view with ease because the drama does not focus in front of him, it revolves around him. Clifford finally pulls out two tickets for a show Marion had once expressed an interest in seeing (he had gone out of his way to collect two returned tickets). However, no sooner does he reveal his trump cards than Marion reveals that such an evening will be impossible because it is the 'first recital of Frankie's ballet class'. In addition, just as Marion says 'class', Ellen cries out 'Mother, I can't find the scarf anywhere.' The dramatic incident that surrounds him is condensed: the interruption to his flow by this disappointing news would be enough for Clifford, without having the disappointing news also interrupted. Clifford affects a moment of stillness, by moving to hold Marion; the film cuts to close-up, and for the moment, the rest of the house is shut out. When Clifford says, 'Look, I am very, very grateful you were born ... This is the one day in the year that belongs exclusively to you', it is neither unctuous nor gushing. MacMurray invests the lines with a persistence that is loving: they are delivered eagerly but with constancy and tenderness. Yet Clifford's effort to regain intimacy with Marion is typically thwarted; the film adopts a perspective from inside the walk-in wardrobe, as Frankie runs into their bedroom behind them. The little girl pirouettes in the bright light of their bedroom – 'Will my hair glitter across the footlights?' – transforming their private space into a theatrical stage, while they watch in the shadows (kept at the bedroom's edge). Yet this is but a flicker of glitter: Frankie quickly exits off-stage left, Marion pulls away from Clifford once again, and Ellen also runs from the mirror where she has been arranging her scarf. Forced for a few seconds to be a spectator of his own bedroom, Clifford must now return to the landing.

He is still holding the bunch of flowers that have yet to find a home and they encapsulate his transitional state. They are one of several objects around the house – telephone, sash, scarf – which the performers use to direct their performances, without necessarily directing their attention to the objects. (Indeed, MacMurray does not direct any exasperated looks to the flowers, or adopt any similar behaviour which might overstate their presence and disrupt the delicate weighting of elements; as a consequence he does not exaggerate his humiliation, or collapse his movements between rooms into farce.) In the final moments of this sequence, Clifford attempts to use the tickets to re-connect with his family, offering each of them the opportunity to accompany him to the show. All have other plans, and he catches each of them as they are in the process of leaving the house. Vinnie puts on his coat and hat, while keeping his back to his father; Marion runs down the stairs and is in the middle of pulling on her gloves; the home help, already dressed to depart, makes a quick telephone call before she leaves. It is their involvement with the everyday items of departure, rather than their outright refusal of his offer, which most potently conveys the rejection. Their involvement with these items is merely preparatory but it is precisely their habitual manner that emphasises their own things and their own routines – always their own, and always everyday – and which subtly announce the worlds from which Clifford is excluded.

The second main sequence of the film, following immediately on the heels of the family's departure, is a companion piece to the previous sequence; both Fred MacMurray and Barbara Stanwyck depend on the first period in the home resonating into the next sequence, so that they may play off it, without needing to overtly acknowledge it. The performers rely on the habitation of spaces from the previous sequence, the patterns and rhythms within those spaces, and the significance they have accrued. The first sequence has been characterised by bustle, and continuous movement, but after the family's departure from the house, the film dissolves to Clifford eating alone in the kitchen, and the quality of his stillness is established by contrast. Their departure has condemned him to domesticity; he is in the kitchen, he wears an apron, and he rescues an overheating percolator from the stove. The doorbell rings while he lifts and carries the hot coffee and the interruption of his task draws more attention to the task (the bell does not ring, for example, while he is sitting eating). It creates a sense of disturbance and continues the pattern of interruption and diversion within the home.

Clifford's activity in the kitchen, however slight in terms of screen time, and however passing – indeed because it is slight and passing – show the performer to be involved in a location, a world, rather than simply acting out a dramatic progression. The drama of incident and event enters into and progresses through that location and that world. Because the doorbell rings after he has picked up the percolator, it opens up the possibility of the performer travelling to the door with percolator in hand, and rhymes with him having to carry the bunch of flowers. Perfunctory tasks are rendered discontinuous, but inescapable, and encapsulate the sense that Clifford is unable to carry out his own wishes in his own time. His carrying of the percolator is mundane and becomes significant in the larger scheme of his actions. The carrying of the flowers was also a rather uneventful activity carried along within the stronger currents of movement. Considered together we see prevailing aspects of character and situation.

Clifford opens the door, and a woman stands a few yards back from the entrance; she faces away from the doorway, and as the door is opening, she is turning. That we see her first from inside the house, and have not been privy to her approach, or her preparations, directs and controls our curiosity. Has she stepped back from the door (if the door opens, I mustn't be too close, too soon)? Is she leaving and not waiting long enough (I'm having second thoughts)? Is she feigning casualness (I've just dropped round, if he's in he's in)? She steps out of shadow and into the light coming from the interior and her sudden appearance at the door suggests a magical visitation, with the puff-of-smoke already dispersed. (Was the house emptied before her visit by ethereal powers? Has Clifford unconsciously summoned her during a reverie in the kitchen?) Yet, despite this, Barbara Stanwyck refrains from wilful mysteriousness, and instead keeps her character's presence delicately suggestive. The suggestiveness is ordinary, gentle and carefully directed; she keeps her head still while her eyes scan his face with an appreciative inquisitiveness (the film holds them both in shot at a medium distance so that to catch the movement of her eyes we must match the sensitivity of her survey). The sequence as it continues depends on Stanwyck managing the relationship between intimacy and distance: her character remains open and invites trust, while withholding information about herself and her motivations. The area around the entrance acts as a suitable location to distil a recurrent tension in Stanwyck's performance of holding back even as she reaches out, and reaching out as she holds back, thoughtfully negotiating her connection.

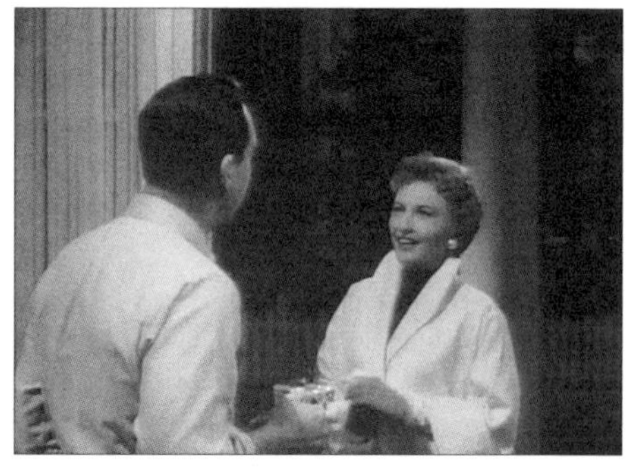

Her attire has angular features, a touch severe but also crisp and clean, neat and honed (it later emerges that she is a fashion designer). Her white coat, thick cut, has a long collar that stiffens as it rises towards the back of her neck. The central break in the coat produces a sharp V out of her black polo-neck underneath. Everything is securely mature, firm and contained, and controlled. Her cuffs are large and heavy and might have flapped clumsily, but instead sit sturdily upon her wrists. Her hair, tightly curled and set, is no doubt the product of much effort, but seriously managed, rather than vainly cherished. A triangular flat hat that could so easily have been incongruously perched is made to nestle snugly, without jostle, close to her hair. Maybe her appearance is too composed, especially in the context of her surprise visit. Signs of tension are mostly hidden, but the manner in which she holds her handbag reveals some strain in the self-possession:

she keeps it close to herself, tightly clutched to her waist, one hand above, one below, like a squirrel jealously guarding her livelihood. This aside, she has an invigorating command of nonchalance. After she has stepped into the light, Clifford takes some time to recall who she is. 'Have I changed that much?' she asks, and then he realises – 'Norma Miller' – and she laughs cheerily, and endearingly. Entertained by his failure to recognise her immediately, she also uses the opportunity to be carefree. So the moment won't freeze, she releases a warm breeze which wafts them both into the house.

A telling gesture then occurs, and the depth of its significance is achieved by its placement. It occurs just inside the house, near the stairs, the site where Clifford has watched his son ignore him on the telephone, and where his youngest child spun around him, and away from him, into the kitchen. He is still holding the percolator and wearing an apron, so Norma pats him on the arm, and Clifford, immediately receptive, turns. She nimbly removes the garment, and holds it out for him to collect. Having at last received a simple and gentle piece of attention, he moves away from her, back into the kitchen, while her arm remains held out, suspended in the air. With her body slightly drawn forward, the hand that made brief contact seems to take the weight, while also floating, seeming light. Captivated as he departs, a gesture of handing back becomes one of reaching out; and her deftness at removing the apron only intensifies the gesture of yearning.[1] A swift moment of affinity quickly becomes one of distance. We know nothing of their past at this moment, and for its length the film discloses little concrete information (no flashbacks, for example). The film does not provide a direct presentation, or explanation, of a past that is too potent

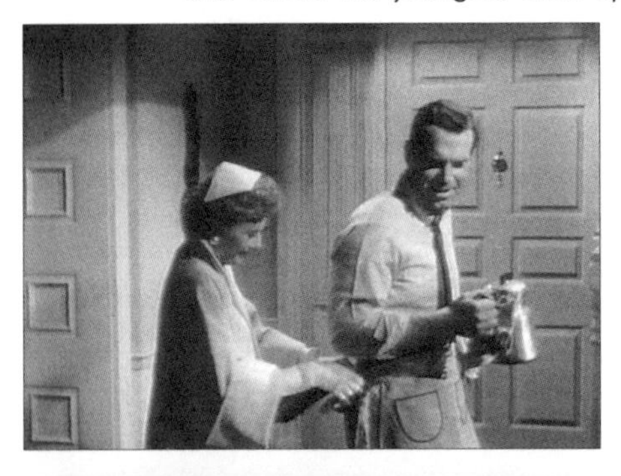

and too indistinct. The performers provide more indirect, yet appropriate, ways of communicating their characters' pasts. Stanwyck economically expresses a life's regrets in the gesture. Norma longs for Clifford and a domestic life, but is unable to grasp them. The film uses the same kitchen to suggest both of their alternative lives: only a few moments before, his family all departed, Clifford was trapped in the kitchen, wishing to be away from it; now as he returns to the same location, all Norma's unfulfilled desire is channelled towards it. Clifford's move away from Norma has a similar aspect to Marion's moves away from him: as Clifford and Norma realise a moment of significance it is already moving away from them. The context of the household setting allows the ordinary, domestic moves of one character – needing to get on – to break a moment of singular significance for the other character.

Norma's suspended gesture seems to stir the music, which intensifies her feeling of loss, and, as she turns and moves through the hallway, it establishes a tenor for her connection with the house. Stanwyck interacts with the familiar space and draws out fresh aspects. This was the space where Ellen and then Vinnie spoke on the telephone. They took the house for granted – and their telephone calls focused them towards places and persons outside it – but Norma moves through it, experiences it, and surveys it as if she were trying to imagine his life *and* an alternative one of her own. This creative engagement transforms the area from an everyday place to one that is charged and filled with shadows (with most of the family absent from the house, the lights have been turned off). For Norma it is a place of concealment and discovery; Ellen and Vinnie find it familiar, and therefore have no need to find it at all. Later she says, 'Oh the house is beautiful – warm, cheerful – just as I had imagined it.' This is an important line of dialogue because up to this point the house has not been verbally acknowledged or registered as a dramatic concern by the characters, even though the relationship between performer and house has been pressing. She moves towards him and continues, '...the kind you always wanted', and she conveys ambiguous intent: is this a statement of truth, an inquiry, or a suggestion? Has Clifford failed lately to see that the house genuinely is 'warm' and 'cheerful', or is it just as *she* imagines it ('just as [she] had imagined it')? Stanwyck's ability to perform an intense and intelligent engagement with her surroundings is facilitated by her talent for transforming and restoring: a talent, perhaps, for generous interpretation.

Norma's turn earlier at the front door initiates a pattern of turning *towards* him, and attending to him, whereas the other characters always turn away. Clifford's house is a theatre, full of exits and entrances, endless and manic preparatory scurrying, last-minute rehearsals, frantic searches for costumes: never enough time. Their constant immersion in tasks is an indication of their deeper inattention. They are always moving away, into the future, or elsewhere, always preparing, and always purposive. Norma can be still. She has a deft relationship to the present, and to the immediacy of feeling in any moment. Stanwyck's lingering gaze expresses the strength of Norma's awareness and attention.

Norma has the capacity to search and discover new aspects, but she simultaneously uses her searches and discoveries to hide herself. Her investigations into his house allow the management of her own disclosure. Later, they face each other in the lounge with a big armchair between them over which she drapes her arms. Her position of relaxation is amply shielded. Her control of casualness continues after they declare how wonderful it is to see each other: she halts this frankness by turning and drifting deeper into the lounge, and continuing her inspection of the house. She is unlikely to be worried by the frankness alone, needing rather to influence its course, and this will be usefully contrived by a genuine piece of curiosity. Her look away to look around also presents an opportunity to turn back, when the time feels right. When he says, 'It's the best surprise I've had in years', she turns rather sharply as if she cannot hide her excited response. It also appears, however, that she is keen to mark the moment by showing her face – now. Her initial retreat opens up a new chance for engagement and sets up an effective return.

Norma's poised performance graces Clifford's theatre. She is able to experiment with Clifford, get closer while she keeps some distance, and remain generous to him. Ultimately, her intentions may be flirtatious rather than committed, but Stanwyck performs it at no cost to the character's intensity of feeling. Norma's flirtatiousness is intimate with seriousness (it may substitute for loss, or protect her from it). Frustration, hurt, loneliness, boredom and loss – all these forceful emotions are contained in the sequences, but the performers do not stand centre-stage eager to impress us with their capacity to visibly embody them. MacMurray, for example, does not huff and puff with the kids, drop his head in his hands at being left alone, or over-charm Norma. The performers are not over exposed or put under a pressure that might force them to demonstrate. Their dramas are dispersed around the house, so they remain faithful to the emotions we displace.

A place to sit: The Cobweb

Dr McIver (Richard Widmark), head of a psychiatric hospital, is sunk in a large yellow armchair and surrounded by gloomy shadows, in his study at home. Filling most of the widescreen frame, the chair appears enlarged and stretched, and he appears spread against it. McIver's figure is thick set and stiff and he is usually ever so upright; now buried deep within the chair he is uncommonly languorous. Suddenly a light is cast on him. The film cuts to show his wife, Karen (Gloria Grahame), standing at the frame of the doorway to their brightly lit bedroom. Her thick, white bathrobe falls away exposing one naked shoulder like a huge gash, and her human flesh bleeds through the material. By displaying her naked shoulder, she may wish to revive McIver's interest in her or petulantly disturb his decorum, or arouse him as she disturbs him. She may simply be coming undone. She tightly clutches both sides of the robe at her chest, trying to hold things together and hold herself in, even as she desires to be released. She wishes to protect (her sense of) her sexuality, but by using it as provocation, she puts it at risk. While her body remains unjustly impris-

oned within her robe, with her shoulder eager to escape, McIver sits in merciless judgement. Thus immersed, he maintains a languid indifference and aggravates with detachment. His deep voice emerges from deep in the chair; deliberately unmoved, he deliberately delivers, 'I'd be home more Karen, if there were more to come home to.'

McIver and the chair dominate the frame, a focal point for the dramatic situation, condensed and intense. This contrasts to McIver's positions in the previous sequences in *The Cobweb* (Vincente Minnelli, 1955) where he takes his place within a widescreen frame that encompasses a range of furniture and character activity, and where dramatic movement is spread more evenly across the frame. After the varied arrangements established in the previous sequences, the frame now only has one piece of furniture within its wide expanse, and the composition seems to be under strain. McIver's position is *stressed*, and caps a pattern, developed through a series of three scenes, where his engagement with three different women is negotiated by way of his relationship to household furniture, and especially chairs. In the first of this series, McIver returns with Meg Rinehart (Lauren Bacall), a colleague of his at the psychiatric home (in charge of arts and crafts), to her apartment. Everything about Meg is unadorned, and has the appearance of unaffected authenticity. She carries a brown paper grocery bag with food supplies as she ascends the outdoor steps to her home. Her clothes fit efficiently, and refuse decoration: straight trousers rather than skirts or dresses, lines rather than curves, and muted colours. With his relationship to Karen in trouble, McIver is becoming increasingly attracted to Meg. She is contrasted to his wife, and she fits with the qualities that have become paramount for him: she is perfectly suited – straight (forward), without fuss, and apparently in control.

Indeed, the film explores psychology through aspects of physical consonance. McIver's desires, or Meg's traits, are not explicitly spoken of by the performers, but instead are insinuated through their congruence with domestic furniture and décor. The psychiatric hospital itself is a large country house and the main plot line in the film concerns the replacement of drapes, and the entanglements that ensue from the preferences of the different characters regarding these drapes. The psychological problems of the patients within the hospital are made explicit; their symptoms are striking and repeatedly commented upon. The film deliberately categorises their conditions, contrasting them to the hospital staff and their families, whose psychological problems are equally potent, but less clinical, and apparently less appropriately considered within an institutionalised medical discourse. Appropriately, therefore, their problems are explored through the performers' ordinary, even incidental, interactions with the settings outside the hospital.

Meg has only recently moved into the flat and as they enter it, they appear at the right edge of the frame. The rest of the screen is filled with scattered objects, half unpacked and the widescreen spreads it out, transforming the ordinary clutter into widespread disarray. After the death of her husband, Meg is trying to construct a new life in a new location and although the mess of removal is to be expected, it represents her transitional and unsettled state. The flat contrasts to McIver's home which, in accord with many of his desires, is ordered and unruffled. Yet at the same time Meg's disordered flat, less set in its ways, offers a space which may satisfy other emerging desires for McIver. The exposed brick-wall interior is representative of this newly conducive space: painted whitish blue, it harmonises with his grey jacket, and is appropriately cool; and its rough earthiness contrasts to his home, where the smooth cosmetic decoration now seems more in keeping with Karen's strained efforts at glamour.

The wooden chair (for a single person) that Meg offers him has been made by her and shares many of her characteristics: it is made from traditional material but has a modern simplicity (a touch sparse, perhaps?); it has slim parts, a straight back, and is firm (a touch hard, perhaps?) The straight lines of Widmark's physique and chair meet each other: his square upper body – whose surfaces are neatly planed off by the sharp cut of his formal jacket – smoothly slots into place ('This thing is comfortable', he muses). His arms are parallel to those of the chair, and his legs bend evenly at a right angle. In the yellow armchair, he loses his shape, and is kept back. Buried within it, he shows what is buried within him. Meg's chair keeps him alert and upright; it staunchly supports the public figure.

The relationships between performer, furniture and the room are maintained and the film refuses to separate, or isolate, the elements by cutting. Yet it is the widescreen framing which accentuates the sense of a wider view, and the result is that many of the performers' most revealing gestures are of low prominence in the frame. Meg and McIver sit close together, but despite their adjacency, their chairs do not directly face each other; they are able to look across or past the other person, avoiding any sustained and uncomfortable eye contact. Meg shifts forward and back in her seat, and tinkers, seemingly needlessly with various cigarettes and ashtrays. Meg's gestures reflect the gathering sexual tension: she straightens her neck, plays with the back of her hair, and pulls up her knees, as if locking herself in. Bacall performs them with stealth, however: her fiddling is not fidgety, her restlessness restrained, and each of her actions is rather exactly executed. Her nervous gestures are calmed, checked, and slowed, as if they were at once involuntary *and* subject to conscious control. Bacall's performance is aided by the dissipating effect of the framing: the camera's reasonable distance from the performers combined with the (wide) distance between the left and right boundaries of the frame. The gestures are kept open to our view, while the lack of emphasis upon them, subordinated by the widescreen, faithfully evokes Meg's desire for them to be hidden. Indeed, McIver may recognise her movements, but he may not, and the shot reminds us that such gestures may be quite prevalent, and yet remain unseen.

Where, when and how the performers sit is crucial to the film's dramatic arrangements. Meg and McIver are seated in symmetry on firm wooden chairs. At this time in their life, they share many of the same *positions* (especially with regard to the clinic) but rather than having a supple mutuality, their compatibility rests rather too strictly on how they are presently situated. Furthermore, because Meg professionally admires McIver, he can be comfortable with his position, and need not assert his authority. Authority is exactly what he asserts in the following scene with Vicki Inch (played by the aged Lillian Gish). As a doctor who believes in modern methods – personified by Meg's streamlined efficiency – he is somewhat out of place in Vicki's front room full of antique furniture, ornamental clutter and imposing portraiture. His need to reprimand her is dramatised in terms of him trying to control a room that, like Vicki, is antagonistic, unwieldy and alien (of another age). He pulls up an old rocking chair so that he may face her, and direct himself at her, while also maintaining his distance (he remains at the left edge of the frame). This becomes the doctor's chair from which he administers and dispenses, while she must sit still: he orders her to 'sit down' a few times, and forbids her from making moves that may control how he treats her. She does as she is told, sitting on an upright dining chair, correctly, and reluctantly, to order; she is pinned down, and pushed up against the right side of the frame.

Unfortunately given the opportunity to rock, McIver cannot quite keep still in his chair. He moves to adopt a new position, standing over her, towards the middle of the dining table that separates them. He starts tapping his fingers on a light blue object, glacial and spherical – it is the head for Vicki's wig – that sits upon the table. He moves away from the head, to lean on a large armchair, and to address Vicki from yet another angle – but then he returns. Despite managing to get her hairpiece on her head just in time before McIver's rude intrusion to her home, he nevertheless indirectly exposes this area of insecurity. He apologises to her for affairs being 'tangled up' and strokes the upper rim of the head; he then asserts, that contrary to her feelings, 'the patients make the drapes', and his thumb lightly taps it with each word, until 'drapes', whereupon his fist concludes matters with a thump. The psychiatrist tries to get to grips with her mind by prodding it, caressing it and knocking it. Its symbolic role, as substitute for her head, might be uncalled for were it not that McIver also seems to need it. Aside from tapping Vicki's sensitivities, his hands display the indirect symptoms of his efforts to speak directly.

Unlike the previous scene with Meg, both the object and the hand gestures are accentuated. The head's importance was prominently declared in the opening shot of the scene. It sat with wig asleep upon it, close-up, magnified, dominating the right foreground of the widescreen. Vicki's house is a new location for the film, and the head makes for a bizarre point of emphasis in an establishing shot. Vicki comes out of the background to answer McIver at the door and picks it up en route. The object's function is marked for the viewer whereas McIver seems unaware of its use; it is merely another of Vicki's obscure paraphernalia. Our attention to it highlights his inattention (he looks at it, he does not recognise it) despite him being drawn to it magnetically. The opening shot, therefore, establishes the pivot around which McIver, unmindful, will try to handle the space. Once attuned to the significance of the performers' seating, we may be alert to when they cease to sit, when they get up, and why; indeed, we conceive of standing up and moving around as *not* sitting. McIver thinks that getting up and walking around controls Vicki and the situation. He takes up a variety of positions, with the head as a focal point, from which to project at her, and *get at* her. Yet his movements also indicate his inability to maintain a secure position from which to speak, and sit still with her.

The problem of placing himself is developed, and deepened, in the next sequence when he tries to confront his wife Karen. With Meg, he sits steadily, balanced in the middle of the widescreen frame, and yet he sits upon her rather makeshift chair. He is forced to rush off to sort out Vicki and the drapes, but this need is representative of the larger situation: he can only temporarily situate himself in this way with Meg and, like her belongings, he is out of place until things get sorted out. With Vicki, he moves around the room even though she sits still. Now Karen returns home from her night with Dr Devanal (Charles Boyer). Staccato hooting and screeching on the soundtrack, an appropriately disruptive fanfare, contemptuous of any clean melodic lines, accompanies her entrance into the house. Inside the house, McIver and his son (Tommy Rettig) – the young boy wears a dressing gown that could easily pass for an adult's velvety smoking jacket – are sitting in the foreground facing each other playing chess, on high, straight-backed chairs. Through their symmetry, they present a stable picture of patriarchal formality, which Karen will nevertheless unsettle. Grahame's physical movements, interrupting the frame's harmonious compositions, express Karen's psychological unrest. Concurrently, Widmark adopts positions which try to re-establish lines (and lines of contact). Karen enters the front door at the back-right of the frame, slams it, shouts 'Goodnight' and goes up the stairs on the left side of the frame. As she stands at the top of the stairs, he moves across to the bottom of them, creating a centre point on a line between son and mother. She breaks the line and scampers upstairs, refusing to be composed like her husband.

Karen's distress is also conveyed through contrasts in colour, as the performer clashes with the décor. She enters their bedroom, all soft violet and lilac, muted and shimmering, purples becoming light blue. The same décor reflects different grievances (and support both performers): too airily feminine, insubstantial and cosmetic, for him perhaps; too cool and clinical now for her. She throws off her black coat, kicks off her black shoes, and chucks her black bag against the mauve, satin-sheet double bed (unlike the McIvers it is worryingly undisturbed): her pent-up passion splatters the pastels (while the stabbing music surges). Her husband enters – 'I've been waiting three hours Karen, I'd like to talk to you' – in his dispassionate grey suit. Inside the shower, she urgently washes away her unclean encounter with Devenal. The orange, fleshiness of her upper body and scarlet lips burn against the impervious blue, shiny tiles and metallic rims and is a reminder that even incandescent nakedness may fail to re-ignite a refrigerated marriage.

Grahame is not afraid to display Karen's pathologies flagrantly, and her manic presentation of frustrated sexuality bravely invites the irritation of the audience. Yet her conflicts with colour, and her tussles within the composition, have such vigour that we may enjoy her behaviour as an energetic rebellion against those domestic aspects that rein her in. Even in the shower, she is boxed up, and the widescreen frame is rigidly divided so that when McIver enters he neatly takes his place in his own cordoned-off square. He leaves the shower room, and this gives further excuse for Grahame to shout and squeal to be heard above the running water. The (high) pitch of her performance only further marks out the smooth and dulcet tone of Widmark's, sounding calm and reasonable. In contrast to him, she refuses to sit still. Earlier, he sat at the end of the bed with arms outstretched by his side and his palms resting on the sheets, a safe seating position, balanced and easily secure (about what he knows – 'What were you drinking for, you know alcohol dilates the capillaries?'). She moves over to her dressing table where she looks in the mirror to pin up her hair, perching on the stool with one leg, unbalanced and insecure (about what she knows – 'oh go write a book if you know so much'). The noisy manifestations of her unhappiness are exacerbated by his undemonstrative behaviour, more socially acceptable, but equally a symptom, and serenely invasive.

Widmark sympathetically presents both sides of the professional male's split personality: a talented and forward-thinking doctor, caring and committed in public, who too easily becomes cold and detached in the domestic sphere. One long take highlights an important sequence of his movements. As Karen sits at her dressing table, brushing her hair before a large mirror, he berates her from the side. Her resistance frustrates him, and he is forced to move, wandering out of shot, but reappearing in the reflection. He repeats the move during their argument returning to her side and then back behind her, so we see him again in the mirror. His movement in and out of reflection ensures his repositioning is emphatic. It is commonplace for mirrors to show aspects of split identity but more marked here is the way that his psychological difficulties are

shown through his inability to find a position to address her. The fact that she is also reflected throws up the problem of which version of the woman he is addressing. As well as width, widescreen is conducive to enhanced depth (and is enhanced further here by the mirror); the width of the frame cannot help him so he moves to the middle of the shot and room. When Karen screams in anger and bashes her hairbrush down on the dressing table, he says, 'Rosie's asleep.' We are still viewing him through the mirror, and through it, we see him move deep into the background of the shot to close the door. The open door has been present in the reflection throughout and allowed their argument to remain fraught in its potential to *disturb* the children. She is dismissive of his protection of them, and tells him that when Rosie was asked at school what she wanted to be when she grew up, she replied: 'A patient!' Now at last the film cuts as if to catch McIver, deliberately and suddenly, bereft in the wide image. It unseats him.

In all the films discussed in this chapter, performer and place find and reveal each other, so that the discovery of location is inseparable from the investigation of psychology: the performers look to their environment to realise their characters. Discreet and considerate disclosure of personality replaces definite announcement and revelation. And as the performers move around a location, elaborating their state and situation, they complicate the direction of the narrative...

3 PLOT

Whose plot?: Secret Beyond the Door

Many Hollywood films – especially thrillers – base their drama on heavily-plotted scenarios and some may appear over-determined and contrived. *Secret Beyond the Door* (Fritz Lang, 1948) could be regarded as obvious, crude and even banal. Beyond a standard need for generic plot conventions, it looks to have an attachment to cliché that is without irony, and an earnestness that brings it close to comedy. It is a story about a man, a husband, suffering from an acute Oedipal crisis where each reminder of a trauma makes him at best distant and at worst murderous. The wife, who is under threat from the husband, pieces together the puzzle – the pieces of which present a clutter of cartoon psychoanalytic symbolism – and forces him to face his trauma, and in a revelatory piece of therapy, releases him.

As the subject here is plot, it is worthwhile to set it out more fully. The film begins with Celia (Joan Bennett), a sophisticated urban woman from New York, standing in a church at her wedding ceremony. In voiceover, she narrates the story of how she got to this point. She has a close relationship with her brother and is on the verge of marrying a considerate and conventional lawyer, Bob (James Seay). While in Mexico, she meets Mark Lamphere (Michael Redgrave), an architect. They seem to be meant for each other. On their honeymoon, also in Mexico, just before they make love, Celia locks the bedroom door to keep him waiting while she prepares herself. Mark suddenly deserts her claiming he has an urgent business meeting. This distresses Celia, but he eventually sends her a message which declares his love and tells her to meet him at his country home in Levender Falls. Caroline Lamphere (Anne Revere), Mark's sister, meets her at the station. Mark is still not back from New York. She mentions that Mark has already been married to a woman called Eleanor, now deceased, and has a son David (Mark Dennis), information Celia did not know. Celia will now inhabit the bedroom that once belonged to Eleanor. Celia meets Miss Robey (Barbara O'Neil) who also lives in the house and wears a scarf that covers the left-hand side of her face. (Miss Robey has been scarred from a fire but in fact her face has healed; she keeps up the appearance because she loves Mark and hopes to maintain his sympathy.) Later Celia meets Mark at the station and they kiss, but something startles him and he yet again recoils. During a big housewarming party for Celia, Mark does a tour of various rooms he has recreated within his house. The rooms are the locations of famous murders. One room, marked number seven on the door, is not included in the tour. Celia is rather perturbed at Mark's hobby especially given that there is some mystery over the nature of Eleanor's death. Mark is estranged from David and resents Celia's efforts to encourage rapprochement. With Mark's behaviour becoming increasingly distant and hostile, she endeavours to find out the Secret Beyond the Door.

She copies the key with candlewax from one of the candles on the mantelpiece in her room (and Mark notices that one candle is shorter and is bothered that it 'breaks the symmetry'). One night she enters the room. She finds a copy of Eleanor's bedroom, but then notices that one candle is shorter than the other. This is her room ... and therefore the eventual site of her...! Terrified she runs out of the house, but gets lost in the foggy grounds. A man approaches her out of the fog. The film fades to black as Celia screams. It stays black for ten seconds. After this long break, the film eventually continues and, in a fantasy sequence, Mark is putting himself on trial for the murder of Celia. Celia, however, is still alive, has returned to the house and is standing in the bedroom. She says that she wanted to leave but their love was more important. She

would rather be dead than without him. Mark yet again disappears but returns to find Celia in room number seven. On the verge of strangling her with a scarf, she makes him confront his past, and he tells the story. He was obsessed with his mother. It was a beautiful day and she was picking lilacs. That night she was going out and he was distressed so she promised that when he was ready for bed he could come to her and she would read to him. Unfortunately, his bedroom is locked from the outside, and Mark becomes hysterical, forced to watch with envy from the window as a man picks up his mother to take her out. He screamed and crushed the lilacs. Marrying this story with information she had received earlier from Caroline, Celia tells him the truth. It was Caroline, not his mother, who locked him in his room (for a prank). The traumatic incident explains his irrational behaviour with Celia: the locked door in Mexico triggered his memories, and his reaction on kissing her at the station was caused by seeing lilacs in her lapel. Although prone to violent impulses therefore, he did not kill Eleanor, and does not want to kill Celia. The confrontation with his past and the revelation that his mother did not lock him in his room seems to release Mark. Meanwhile Miss Robey has set fire to the house. Mark and Celia narrowly escape and return for a second honeymoon in Mexico where they agree to continue to help Mark overcome his traumas.

Attention to performance will enable us to take the plot summary and explore the actual presentation of the drama: to *flesh* out the synopsis. The synopsis implies that most of the plot elements of the film and their intrigue revolve around a concern with the mind of Mark.[1] Yet, running consistently throughout the film is Celia's voiceover, giving us access to *her* mind. As Celia sits still and straight-backed upon her bed, waiting, we hear her voiceover: she says, 'Time seems to stand still when you wait for everyone else to sleep'. There is a tension between her calm and composed outward appearance and her intense inner voice. Mark drew attention to this divergence when they first conversed in Mexico, and his perspicacious insight cements their early attachment. He says that she is a sleeping beauty waiting to be awakened:

> ...you aren't what you seem to be. There is something in your face I saw once before, in South Dakota, in the wheat country ... just before the cyclone. The air has a stillness, a flat, gold, shimmering stillness. You have it in your face, the same hush before a storm.

> The way you smile it's like the first breath of wind bending down the wheat. I know behind that smile is a turbulence.

She listens to him, barely moving, while her voiceover reflects the rumblings of this 'turbulence': 'I heard his voice and then I didn't hear it anymore – the beating of my heart was louder – this is what I hunted for all those foolish years in New York.' Having achieved the divergence between her demeanour and her internal thoughts, Bennett could have rested and failed to substantiate the voiceover. During threatening moments, as she waits to discover the secret beyond the door, Bennett does not simply collapse her internal feelings into suffering or distress. Her vocal manner is deep and breathy, rounded and smooth, and never high-pitched. Sensuously rhythmic, it modulates, caresses and nurtures even her most anxious thoughts. She contains the turbulence as if relishing her passion on the verge of release. The voiceover allows her to keep thoughts courteously to herself while she impolitely whispers: eagerly murmuring, illicitly, close to the viewer's ear.

Given that the film's generic framework is that of the Persecuted Wife Thriller,[2] one of the film's distinctions is to present Celia as sophisticated and mature. She is not an inexperienced and wide-eyed young girl, and Bennett presents Celia's whirlwind romance and marriage as a particularly determined surrender. Accustomed to keeping both feet securely on the ground, she is more than ready to be swept off them. Before meeting Mark, her passion has been too safely internalised with no promise of help because she outwardly appeared to be undisturbed. Bennett is adept at performing Celia's direct and lucid sociability and her friendly and respectable flirtatiousness that protects other, maybe less decorous, aspects of her sexuality. Her achievement is to characterise such personality traits as concealing but not duplicitous. She shows that a trait can mask without being a superficial veneer, or a deliberate pretence, and this makes such traits resilient and reassuring (for her and for others). Celia's psychological dislocations are more significant for the film than Mark's partly because they are common in ordinary life, but also because they are uncommon in the thriller genre. They are unsuitably undramatic and unlike Mark's cannot be easily plotted: they provide no obvious mystery that needs solving, they have no symptoms which are threatening, they are not rooted in an eventful trauma, they do not rise to crisis and they cannot be as deliberately unravelled. Paradoxically, because her character's concerns are not thrilling, she can use the thriller framework to permit an appropriately veiled dramatisation.

Bennett explores her character's psychology while she and the film appear to be dealing with Mark's. In the search and discovery of the room, therefore, she transforms what could amount to a conventionally suspenseful sequence. The house is dark and menacing; she must solve the mystery concerning the room itself; and she must investigate without disturbing Mark! Her behaviour, however, does not seem to reflect these pressing concerns. One would expect her to walk briskly, if carefully, perhaps even scurrying at points, but instead her walk is painfully slow and methodical: down the steps and round the corners and through the corridors with a robotic single-mindedness. The music that accompanies her is at first like a brooding military march to which she walks in step (and then intensifies as if it were her quickening heartbeat). Where is the desperation, and where is the collapse into frantic movement on nearing the destination? The performer paces the film steadily disregarding the plot's urgency.

Celia does not only want to discover Mark's plot, she wants, step by step, to plot her own course. Her torch beam is held on the number seven and then the ring of light only gradually descends to the lock. Although she unlocks the door and slowly eases it open, the beam had seemingly already acted as a key, as if she understood that only her own illumination will unlock the secrets (remarkably, when the torch sat beside her bed upstairs it appeared, silhouetted, like a giant key). Each of her actions is discrete and exact, but she is less caught in a trance than deliberately practicing her own ritual. She recognises that a significant interpretation of the room will not simply arise from its discovery but from realising her approach to it.

Sensitivity to her movement opens up alternative interpretations that reveal a better film.[3] A film may look to have a straightforward plot that determines the direction of the drama. Yet a performance within the film can tell a different story. Our appreciation of a performance may encourage us to reorganise a film's elements and shift our perspective on the action, and this may in turn unlock qualities in a film that appears limited without such an appreciation. The film gives us many symbols – for example shortened candles or taut and flaccid scarves – that threaten to encourage interpretations which are piece-meal and static, drawn from plot summaries, rather than the experience of the film. Appreciating the torch as Celia's personal key, however, arises from an engagement with the movement of Bennett's performance. Such interpretations emerge *and evolve* when we attend to the film as a physical and dynamic entity developing moment-by-moment. When Mark takes the party guests around his collection of rooms there is a rather odd character performed instructively by Anabel Shaw (listed in the credits as 'Intellectual Sub-Deb'). She keeps interrupting his explanations of the murder stories to provide interpretations based on textbook psychoanalysis. She is abrupt, blunt and unattractive in her pompous assertion of knowledge. Her attitudes seem to have removed all the life from her features – bland eyes, mousy hair, pointed nose and harsh voice. Why would a film that seems to have conviction in psychoanalytical reasoning present this character unsympathetically? Perhaps her attentions to psychology are legitimate, but she is too obvious, and too inflexible to be genuinely interested in alternative stories. Throughout the film, many of the flagrant symbols keep confirming Mark's story: the familiar résumé of male repression. A shortened candle represents his fear of castration; the scarf, one moment taut, then flaccid, symbolises the intensity of his sexual excitement and its premature dissipation. The blatancy of these signs distract from the scent: they are unavoidable but unhelpful for following, and experiencing, Celia's subtler symbolic drama.

Indeed, the primary symbol of the door, and the secrets that lie beyond, is something first mentioned by Celia, by the wishing well in Mexico, in relation to herself. She announced that she would 'close the door to a quiet familiar room where I'll be safe ... one door closed and another opened wide and I went through – wind, space, sun, storm – everything was beyond that door.' Now in Levender Falls the door to room number seven opens; the screen is black. Then the beam rises once again, revealing not a room, but a curtain; the curtain is drawn before the stage, and the beam is now transformed into a spotlight. Celia makes her entrance. If the first door, hard, rigid and defensive, asserts male secrecy, the second threshold, pliant, supple, yielding, promises female secrecy. It rhymes loosely with the curtain from which Miss Robey peers to spy on Celia's arrival, and more strongly with the scarf draped by the side of her face, that supposedly conceals her scar. In fact, her face has long since healed, and this deception should be instructive: a secret is being concealed behind the folds of fabric, but not what the plot is leading us to believe. At first, we are led to believe the room is a copy of Eleanor's (and indeed it once was), but Celia soon realises that it is her room. Her findings would be in keeping with the picture of Eleanor as barren (and in keeping with Mark's austere withdrawals from sex). Yet, as she opens the drawers and finds they are bare, and explores behind more curtains, her palms desperately hitting against cold brick, Celia's contact with the room is personally felt. It provides an exaggerated version of what, before being stimulated by Mark, was unreleased in her (and a question seemingly pertaining to Mark's story, 'isn't the room *finished*?', is more suggestive of her own fulfilment). Her declaration therefore, 'It's my room – It's waiting for me', has more meaning than she knows. Bennett complicates the sequence, simultaneously playing it as an external investigation (of Mark), a dip into the aura of Eleanor, and an opportunity to be self-searching: she has been travelling within her own mind, and now touches upon aspects that previously lay dormant.[4]

Is this why the film shows her fleeing the room through the reflection in the large mirror above the mantelpiece? The plot reassures us that she escapes in fear of Mark, but she appears to be running away from a mirror image of herself. In Mexico, on their honeymoon night, she sits in front of an oval dressing table mirror and brushes her hair repeatedly. Her head and shoulders are not merely reflected but captured in the mirror, cut away, framed, like a portrait held before Celia, inviting her to inspect her own pose. To this effect, Bennett adds her own tendency to reflect, so she seems to view the progress of her grooming and the fact of it. Within the thriller genre, one might expect the mirror to show a more pathological split; it would, for example, with its capacities

for duality, cracks or distortions, be the ideal piece of furniture to externally reflect Mark's schizophrenia. Instead, mirrors in the film are associated with Celia's tensions and in Mexico service a rather routine piece of female dissembling. Bennett captures the common strangeness of having to face yourself as you put your face on. Many of the great female performers find opportunity to explore aspects of cosmetic preparation, but usually in the context of more striking presentations of themselves. Throughout, Celia's appearance is classy and sophisticated but because Bennett roots it securely in an identifiable social world – smart, upscale, metropolitan – it carries an air of normality. Celia demurely flirts with movie-star glamour to distinguish herself – as those *outside* movies might do – but is also too straightforward, friendly and unselfish to stand apart and look dramatic. (Her voiceover indicates that she graciously keeps her melodrama to herself.) No performer more endearingly conveys the everyday sense of an attractive woman quietly and humbly *making herself up*.

Celia runs out of the house and her efforts within the grounds seem unconvincingly lacklustre partly because the shot from above artificially asserts the parameters of the space. Celia's capture looks needlessly *set-up*. Yet the film seems to court the look of severe studio constraint so that the scene will appear incredible only if viewed literally. Rather than being unable to escape a real space because she cannot see *where* she is going, perhaps she is unable to escape the fog in her mind. She cannot yet see *why* she is going. The falsity of appearance is in keeping with the disingenuous plot current that leads us to believe that Celia is murdered in the grounds: the ominous male figure; the swirling fog; the fatal scream; the ten-second collapse into darkness; and the trial of Mark. The overt deceit of this current encourages us to re-interpret sections of the film where reassessment is less insisted upon: for example, understanding the whole sequence, from her waiting on her bed to the fade-out, as a psycho-symbolic representation of Celia. Mark re-finds Celia standing at the entrance to her bedroom but leaves the house still afraid of what he might do. We are now left alone in the house with her and this draws

attention to the absence of her customary address to us: the voiceover. Indeed, after the fade-out we never hear it again as if this moment marked the reconciliation of her inner and outer voices. The fade-out is itself like a door closing, and like Celia, who goes beyond Mark's plot and *re-enters* the film (after we thought she was dead), we should now go beyond Mark's plot and enter into a more complete appreciation of the film.[5]

Such an appreciation will allow the Bennett performance to reveal new aspects that were previously, necessarily, subdued. In *Secret Beyond the Door*, the plot is purposeful and demonstrative, and Bennett builds her performance modestly in reaction to it. Her contrasting behaviour creates a suspense that is subtler than that directly asserted by the film's plot. Mark returns to the house and, down in room number seven, he finds Celia. When the door locks behind them, and he sees the lilacs sitting upon the table (put out by Celia), his violent desire is triggered, and he approaches her. When she does not shirk but rises from the chair to face him it is the apotheosis of a behavioural pattern. Throughout, Mark is almost comic in his sudden shifts of moods but Celia, rather than be goaded into grotesquery to win his attention, keeps her poise. The film repeatedly sets up moments where Celia, although faced with a revelation or a shock, does not panic or fret but quickly establishes a matter-of-fact engagement. Miss Robey is set up to be a secretive and possibly threatening presence, but on her first meeting, Celia faces her directly and is civil and respectful; and as she shakes her hand ('goodnight Miss Robey'), she reaches out when we would expect her to cower. Without turning her performance into one of stoical restraint, Bennett keeps Celia steady in a plot pushing to extremes.

One of the pleasures of the film is watching Bennett perform sincerity and maintain it as a plausible and successful attribute in the face of secrecy and duplicity. On her arrival at Levender Falls, when Caroline reveals that Mark has a son, the music comes on all brooding, but apart from widening her eyes, Celia's exterior remains relatively placid (although her voiceover continues to express her concerns). There is no sense that her self-control is anxiously willed. Although Bennett characterises Celia as someone who too easily remains reasonable at the expense of passionate impulse, she also shows her to be comfortable with her placidity, as if it were pleasurably therapeutic. Indeed, the dramatic situations – rather than presenting a threat to Celia – provide a beneficial environment where she may rehearse directness without surrendering to pleasing others or confronting them. Each time the film, true to generic form, delivers another spook, Celia refuses to take it as an attack on her. The performer moulds and shapes the genre situations. The film could easily have been about female self-doubt and paranoia, but instead Bennett fashions a drama of female self-fulfilment.

Her placidity ensures her body must contain tension. Good performances do not need a striking piece of physical behaviour to make a mark. Bennett has a consistency of posture and gesture that gradually distinguishes her presence in the world of the film. Unlike, for example, Stanwyck's arm gesture as she removes the apron in *There's Always Tomorrow*, Bennett rarely performs gestures that are singularly and purposefully expressive in the moment. By the last sequence of the film, she confronts Mark with some characteristic postures: she stands up still and upright and faces him directly. Her arms are either close to her side, hands hovering just above by her waist or else she locks them together under her chest. Often, throughout the film, her arms meet in front of her body; sometimes she is carrying an object – a gift, a towel, or a handbag – providing a practical cover for her hands that masks the tension in her position. This posture is first established at her wedding where she holds a posy. A formality of stance is to be expected here and so appropriately establishes a drama concerning the relationship between the stillness of Celia's external features and the movement of her internal thoughts. This stance is also in keeping with her tendency to adopt symmetrical positions. In Mexico, despite the passionate occasion, she leans on the wishing well with both arms perfectly in accord, remaining even-handed; with Caroline,

after a barrage of new information about Mark, she stands against the fireplace with both her elbows resting on the mantelpiece, holding steady. In general, by standing straight opposite characters, she creates balance. Bennett's range of gesture is successfully constrained, performing a character that is holding her self together.[6] Furthermore, against the stillness of her frame she registers small movements in her features – which act as minor disturbances to the symmetry – like the little curl at the corner of her mouth.[7] Out of this her velvety voice seeps, just enough to regulate an attractive rhythm of speech and provide a touch of friendly seduction to stroke her direct address. On noticing that one candle is shorter than the other Mark says it disturbs him because 'it breaks the symmetry', and no doubt he appreciates Celia because she has the characteristics of his exemplary architectural spaces: a 'felicitous' structure, well-proportioned and harmonious, but with stirrings within.

Appreciating Bennett's performance in turn helps us understand why Michael Redgrave's Mark is an exaggeration of male distance and defensiveness. His performance could face accusations of being stiff and wooden (although acting as a block might be appropriate, if over literal, for a character that is severely psychologically blocked). More importantly, Celia wants to go beyond obvious surfaces, and be responsive to undercurrents and Redgrave suitably refuses, despite his place as a male lead, to appear fluently attractive or charismatic. His mellifluous voice is his most seductive feature and the soft lines drift surreptitiously into Celia's consciousness, flowing out from somewhere beyond his hard surface. Furthermore, everyone in Celia's therapeutic dream world is artificial and strangely mannered. Mark is the prominent example of rigidity in a film that presents a series of severe postures – Caroline, Miss Robey and David – reflecting unbending natures. Celia provides the penetrating variation on this economy of posture: just as Eleanor's frigidity is the negative variant of Celia's inhibitions, the other characters are grotesque versions of her propensity to control her stance. This behavioural coherence means Celia rhymes with the other women. As a woman who is about to share her life with a man, she explores the ways she is related or unrelated to the other women in his life – housekeeper, sister and first wife. In what ways is she not simply a repetition or an imitation? This ensures that the closing moments, as Celia stands up to Mark, are not only about her confronting and healing the fearsome husband, but rather how she fits in with a man she cannot avoid loving and why she is meant for him. In other words, how she stands.

Supporting plots and conjuring plots: Shadow of a Doubt

Shadow of a Doubt (Alfred Hitchcock, 1943) is reaching its climax. Charlie Newton (Teresa Wright) knows that her uncle Charles Oakley (Joseph Cotton) is a serial killer of widows; Uncle Charles is eager to dispose of her before she reveals what she knows. He tries to asphyxiate Charlie by trapping her in the garage with a car chugging out smoke. Inside the house, the family is preparing to go out for the night to hear Uncle Charles' speech to the town of Santa Rosa. He is an honoured guest. Charles turns on the radio and closes the window so that Charlie's screams will not be heard. Herb (Hume Cronyn), a friend and neighbour of Charlie's father Joe Newton (Henry Travers), notices something is wrong, and informs the family. She is rescued just in time. Claiming she will be fine, Charlie urges everyone to go to the speech, while she rests at home. While the family is out with Charles, she tries to ring Jack Graham (Macdonald Carey), the detective who had been investigating Charles (and her possible future lover). She is unable to reach him and therefore must defeat her uncle on her own. She finds the ring that he once presented to her as a gift, and which provides proof of his connection with one of the murdered widows. The family arrives back with invited guests. Preparing for a toast, Charles turns to see Charlie coming slowly down the stairs. He raises his glass and then says, 'Ahhh, here she is, now for my toast.' Then his expression turns grave.

Charlie's descent is very deliberate, and she strains to rest her forearm against the banister to draw attention to it. The camera moves closer and closer to her, eventually settling on her hand.[8] On her fourth finger she wears the ring. The focus is intensified by the sound: everything goes quiet, as if the surrounding activity had been cut away. After this moment of suspension, Charles says, 'Charlie you're just in time for a farewell toast', and then announces that he is leaving.

Charlie now hovers at the bottom of the stairs, barely registering, and almost numb. The plot has reached its climax, and Charlie looks to have successfully achieved her aim. (One of the guests, Mrs Potter – a widow – announces that, like Charles, she was considering travelling to San Francisco the next day too!) There then follows an extraordinary burst of intensity by Charlie's mother, Emma Newton (Patricia Collinge) the effect of which rests partly on its tangential relationship to the drive of the plot concerning Charles and Charlie. The film establishes the moment as an intervention from the sidelines that is nonetheless critical to the concerns of the whole film. Emmy walks in from the dining room, looking stunned. Charles makes up his excuse about needing to leave. 'I'll miss you Emmy', he says and kisses her on the cheek. He turns back to everyone and praises Santa Rosa as a place of 'hospitality and kindness'. Emmy sits down, looks up to Charles and says 'But I can't bear it if you go.' Charlie moves closer, takes a seat and watches her mother's reaction. Emmy continues, ever more distraught: 'It isn't any of the things you've done. It's just the idea that we were together again. I'm sorry. But you see, we were so close growing up, and then Charles ran away and, I got married, and then you know how it is, sort of forget you're you, you're your husband's wife...'

Tears are suspended under her eyes, and her startling intervention remains on the verge while not quite collapsing into uncontrollable weeping. Her eyes stare out, straining to see something within. Collinge conveys the sense of pictures in the mind coming into focus: the memories of her youth and the regrets long ago repressed. First, she kneads her forehead as if rubbing the memories clean. Then she presses her hand against the side of her face as if blocking a spurting wound. When she says, 'I'm sorry', the film cuts to the guests watching on (the admission of a life confined to the family is confessed before an audience that extends beyond the confines of the family). She merges the drama happening inside her with a nervous consciousness of the drama happening before them. The audience within the film intensifies our own discomfort in viewing a fragile woman feeling pain: the nakedness of her emotion. The performer's achievement is to establish a picture of a lifetime in merely a few seconds, but how dispiriting for this character that a few seconds is all it takes. Moreover, the sudden intervention of the outburst within the film contrasts with the day-by-day passing of her life (and her day-by-day life passing her by).

Collinge now expresses intensity and is the focus of attention; suddenly she is at the centre of the drama whereas previously, although often present, she remained humbly at its side. Yet the intensity conveyed so quickly here is not simply a product of her performance contrasting with what has gone before. Collinge makes her intervention look unusual and unexpected, but not anomalous. Her behaviour remains in keeping with her slightly agitated rhythms over matters more mundane. When, for example, she expresses her frustration that Ann (Edna May Wonacott), her youngest daughter, should stop wearing a flower in her ear; or when, just a few moments before her outburst, she is dismayed that, against her better judgement, she continues to make sandwiches where the tomato soaks through the bread (and that her guest should now choose one with cream cheese instead). She has also been adept throughout the film at giving the impression that her worries for other people emerge separately from an immediate engagement with those people. She provides a touching picture of a mother who is caring *and* self-absorbed; whose devotion to others has for too long entailed a private dialogue with her self. Her behaviour throughout could be understood in terms of a serious repression, but the performance does not urge the viewer to press this insight, or treat it as an urgent matter of gravity. Emmy looks content to support her family, while Collinge looks content to fulfil the routine conventions of the supporting player. Her performance happily prompts safe descriptions, that she is eccentric or quirky and possibly a touch whimsical. Therefore aside from what she says in her outburst, it is equally distressing that she is confessing *at all*, and like the guests forced to listen, we have been caught short. She had to announce it before we would seriously attend to it.

The film gives us a privileged glimpse of Emmy's private dialogue immediately after Charlie's 'accident' in the garage. Preparing to travel to Charles' speech, Emmy enters the back seat of the car and the film shows her pondering to herself out-loud about her daughter's recent misfortunes. Collinge combines both sides of Emmy's lack of knowledge. She shows a mother's sixth sense for her daughter's well-being, and our recognition of this sensitivity survives our greater knowledge of the plot: Emmy might have been undermined given that she only has a dim sense of something not being quite right while the viewer is consumed by things being very wrong. At the same time, the failure to notice this gravity earlier is analogous to her failure to recognise her daughter's development as a woman: of Charlie's *growing* situation. Emmy's lack of knowledge of Charlie's story in the film suitably expresses the larger theme of how children may become unknown to their parents. Emmy's unawareness of the plot that surrounds her enables Collinge to express aspects of motherly perspicacity and blindness.

The performer knows the plot but acts as if she knows only a very limited amount. This accomplishment is worth bringing to mind occasionally (even though the performer is rightly eager for us to forget it), because it reminds us how good performers are at authenticating their characters while deceiving us in this way. Collinge maintains the sincerity of Emmy's outburst at the gathering, despite what she, as the performer, really knows about Charles, and what we know about him. 'It isn't any of the things you've done. It is just the idea that we were together again' refers to his charitable deeds in Santa Rosa: her claim is ironic when considered in relation to his killings and the terrorising of her daughter. Furthermore, it is interesting to speculate how different Emmy's outburst would be if it was a response to the knowledge that Charles is a serial killer and not simply to his departure. What would be lost is our sense that her sentiment remains strong and true despite our knowledge of the full facts of Charles and his story (indeed because of the full facts). It establishes the integrity of her outpouring, part of a separate story that has not yet been told.

If the shift of emphasis to Emmy at this moment is telling, the film's move away from her in the middle of her trauma is equally significant. On the word 'married' the film cuts to Charlie looking understandably distressed at her mother's collapse. This develops into more than a reaction shot, however, because the film does not return to show Emmy. Instead, it moves ever closer to Charlie's face and Emmy's devastating words – 'and you know how it is, sort of forget you're *you*, you're your husband's wife...' – are heard from off-screen. The words that describe her disappearance to herself are accompanied by her disappearance from the image. Furthermore, having come up close to Charlie's face, the film then fades to black: 'husband's wife...' and anything more she might have to say is swallowed in the darkness. Her words are allowed to fade away – into a breezy summer morning with attentions back to Mr. Charles Oakley, and with no mention of Emmy or her statement. Her story does not become the focus of the drama, a stimulus for character reaction and response, or a new driving force of the film. A fragment of another story has risen to the surface; it is glimpsed but not laid out, and not told by the film. There is a sense that the outpouring is too traumatic, too disruptive, for the film to progress with it, but perhaps this is also not the story that can, or should, be carefully plotted. It is precisely an undramatic story that will reveal itself in fragments, discontinuous, often buried beneath other people's stories, which are more dramatic. Sudden emphasis on the performer is therefore followed by sudden withdrawal; her sentiment rises only to be quickly subsumed. Collinge performs the emotional crescendo of the scene in the knowledge that she is without the luxury of further elaboration. Yet the skill of the supporting performer is to suggest the story of a life through pieces. They are suitably placed to evoke faithfully the piecemeal perspective we have on certain lives.

All the supporting players in *Shadow of a Doubt*, in different ways, play their performances off the main plot developing between Charles and Charlie. Ann, for example, the youngest daughter of the Newton household, has a usefully tangential relationship to the main action. Ann is another member of the family who has her own particular manner of self-absorption. She is rudely interrupted near the beginning of the film when the telephone rings to inform the Newton household that they have a telegram (from Uncle Charles announcing his visit to Santa Rosa). She is lying on the floor, deeply absorbed in her book (which turns out to be *Ivanhoe*) and eating an apple. She reluctantly moves towards the ringing telephone while never taking her eyes off her book. Then, in a sweet image of the habitual, she finds, bends down and picks up a footstool while never taking her eyes of her book. Even after answering the call, she claims that she refuses to fetch a pencil to record the message because she wants to keep her mind 'free of things that don't matter'. The

telephone call is the first moment in the film that the main plot intrudes on the Newton household. Ann does not want to be disturbed by the telephone, but she also does not wish to be disturbed by the encroaching plot. The film inserts a precocious performance to frustrate our eagerness that the telephone should be answered and the telegram message noted. Her performance gets in the way of the plot's progress, but the film does not simply use her as a delaying device because her behaviour is also unknowingly prescient. Ann is slightly wary of Charles throughout the film, without quite knowing why. Is her behaviour here unconsciously keeping Charles from entering the house?

The performer's skill, again, is to suggest other stories while not allowing them to become the centre of attention. Wonacott's performance of absorption is played as an eccentric distraction. Ann's interventions into the main action – often in the form of single comments – are delivered as studied asides, the product of self-interested analysis, rather than the consequence of involvement. These comments are declared like pronouncements – high-minded and shrill – inviting us to be amused by her, so that we might miss the suggestive perspective that she provides on the action. These proclamations are not quite demonstrations, but odd intimations. When she first sees Uncle Charles, she says, 'You look different', but her comment is unspecific enough not to attract further inquiry from other characters. If she looked more in control of her intentions, she would be like an old(-fashioned) teacher who shuns obvious explanation in favour of indefinite hints (patiently waiting to be understood). Even if the viewer takes these hints, the comedy of her performance ensures that the other characters do not quite take her seriously.

The film establishes a family who are comfortable in each other's presence, but have limited capacities for open communication. The household is close-knit *and* separate. Although each character represents a different variation of self-absorption, which limits their capacity for continuous conversation, they nonetheless create affectionate relationships. At the beginning of the film, Charlie is lying on her bed, staring at the ceiling, and 'thinking' (notably rhyming with Uncle Charles who lies in a similar position in his bedsit) when her father Joe comes up the stairs to stand outside her room. The shot is from inside the bedroom, and the door is slightly ajar. He quietly knocks on the door, and gently pushes it open. Charlie tells her father that things are in a 'rut', nothing happens in the house and that the family 'don't even have any real conversation – just talk.' Joe listens to his daughter's worries but remains at the doorway throughout. He shows care without intimacy, and a generosity of spirit that is without intensity. Joe's position at the doorway encapsulates how he gives his daughter space to express her complaints freely – while showing punctilious respect for a young woman's boundaries – and his nervousness about getting closer. (When Emmy later comes up to join them, she moves immediately into her bedroom, and sits on the bed.)

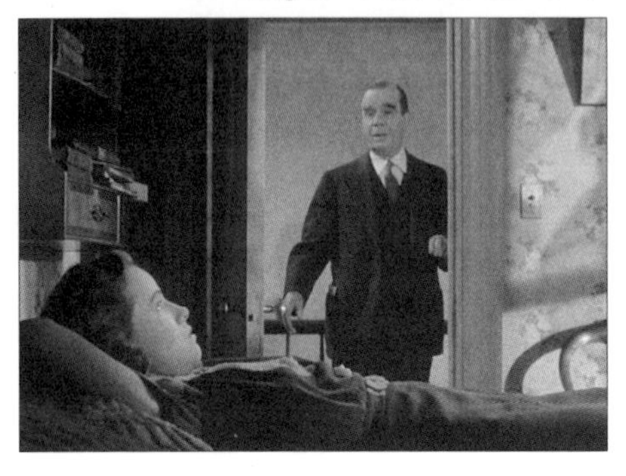

During the conversation, the film cuts to two closer shots of him. The first is when he slips his hand into his pocket carefully, grins slightly and widens his eyes. The shot is barely two seconds long, before the film returns to the wider shot that encompasses Charlie on the bed. The cuts appear to be very carefully inserted, and their deliberateness matches Joe's moves to reposition nervously. They also emphasise that our glimpse of his expressions is privileged: Charlie, immersed in her thoughts, does not notice her father, and the insertions make plain what each family member may be missing in the others. If Collinge successfully enacts possible tensions in motherhood, Travers balances various fatherly traits. Joe is poignantly attentive *and* remote. He listens tenderly *and* humours with a touch of condescension. His responses patiently encourage *and* deflate her ardour. If the cuts are a touch too pointed, it may be because hereafter Joe's nuances will not be pointed up. Travers takes the opportunity to indicate possibilities of Joe's personality that he rarely expresses, and the delicacy of posture and attitude here is enough to infuse his performance over the film.

Like Emmy, Joe has his moment, albeit less intense, to signal some other stories, never properly told. Charlie is at the centre of the main story that receives a full telling, but in keeping with the supporting characters, the complexity of her story is masked by the generic conventions of the thriller plot. Joe's deflationary pricks are rather justified by Charlie's earnestness: although sincere in her feelings, her resignation is performed for her father, her hyperbole – 'I give up, I simply give up ... this family has gone to pieces' – preciously enunciated and announced. This is an early indication of Charlie's behaviour: mature, adult feelings are emerging but they find their expression in the form of girlish play-acting. Indeed, she desires a new play in which she will be free to act. 'I've been thinking for hours', she says, and there is a sense in which (like Celia in *Secret Beyond the Door*) the plot of *Shadow of a Doubt* is spun from her mind. Lying on the bed, waiting, the telephone rings with news of Charles' telegram, as if willed, and the bell spells the beginning of a fairytale. Uncle Charles is the product of a daydream, or a fantasy, summoned to facilitate her move into womanhood. Yet, only dimly aware of her desires, her fantasy is indistinct.

Teresa Wright's performance is remarkably suspended between child and woman, excitedly inviting new experience while seemingly innocent about its sexual motivation. This is reflected in her costume that fails to define her, as she is still yet to fashion herself. When she meets Uncle Charles at the station, she wears a white, stiff, high, tight collar with a ribbon bow which accentuates her thin neck – part uniformed schoolgirl, part spinster old lady. It is Uncle Charles' appearance, therefore, rather than her appearance that embodies the strength of her desire. Charlie bustles to get nearer the train, hands in her coat pocket, and it is from her perspective that we see Charles getting off the train in the distance. On the train, Charles masquerades as sick in order to justify his seclusion, and those now helping him on to the platform drape his overcoat carefully over his hunched shoulders and crooked body. This plot ploy enables Joseph Cotton to transform Charles' arrival into a magical apparition. He moves toward us – and Charlie's eyes – and erects his posture, whisking off his cloak with only one hand, twisting it round effortlessly in a single fluent movement, and hanging it neatly upon his left arm. In the process, he reveals an immaculately fashioned outfit of smart jacket, waistcoat, tie and white shirt – everything is fitting. His walking pace quickens and his cane, first used as a walking stick on which to lean his ailing body, now accentuates his stride, allowing him to march forcefully towards Charlie with a revived rhythm and gusto. Charlie's first view becomes more

like a miraculous conjuring, as if her vision was shaping him, into a model object of desire.

All the family, apart from Emmy, meet Charles at the station; his arrival is set up within the story to be a family affair but bleeds into a private one. Placed within this family situation, Wright more easily establishes Charlie's eagerness for her relative as family love rather than sexual love.[9] Yet, her performance explores the slipperiness of these categories (aided by the plot that presents a man who is practically a stranger to Charlie but who nevertheless is family). Against this background, Wright consummately blurs a child's anticipation with a virgin's restlessness.

The film cuts between them urgently approaching each other on the station platform, and then embracing, evoking the convention of young lovers forced by circumstance to separate, and now joyously reunited. Wright shows the sexual side of the story to us, while hiding it from her character. She displays the sexuality of Charlie's behaviour while keeping it credible that her character would be oblivious to it. The figure of the rarely seen Uncle allows the incest theme to be explored outside the immediate family in territory that is safe and acceptable (but, in fact, remains imaginatively faithful to the way incest within the family may become safe and acceptable). Censorship demands often encourage the creative management of plot situations, but the lack of explicitness is desirable. It prevents the film narrowing into a problem drama about incest, and allows a broader exploration of unconscious sexual currents within families. Back at home, Charles meets Emmy and there is a pointed cut to Charlie, beaming and sighing. The young girl looks up to the older man, and Charlie's expression mixes loving admiration – joyously seeing Charles delighting her mother – with a lover's adoration.

Charlie's fantasy allows her to be stimulated by a strange man while she safely keeps her sexual experimentation within the family. She invites him to sleep in her bed – 'Charlie thought you would be more comfortable here', says Joe – while not actually sleeping *with* him. When he arrives in her room, he picks the one rose that is still only a bud, rips off its head, and places it in his lapel. The gesture that further perfects his appearance according to her desire is also an abrupt deflowering in her bedroom. Wright balances her performance on the cusp of such suspensions but as the film develops, she also performs the struggle to maintain the balance. These achievements of her performance may not be evident if Charles is viewed as an external threat, an intrusion into the cosy world of Santa Rosa. Within this scenario, Wright simply performs a young girl in danger: she is falsely besotted, comes to realisation, and then must find the strength and guile to fight off the villain. The film is happy to encourage this conventional account of the story, in order to mask the alternative account, which needs to be submerged and covert. If the events concerning Charles are alternatively viewed as internally generated, as almost willed by Charlie, then Wright's performance is one of conveying the tensions that revolve around the struggle to keep events within her control. Once again, our appreciation of the richness of performance and our interpretation of the film are mutually dependent. She does not simply want to fight off the presence of Charles; she wants to invite him, manage him, and reject him. Even at the end of the film when she explicitly needs to expunge him, the manner in which she executes it is appropriate to her previous desires to keep him close. For example, she declares her divorce from Charles by re-finding and re-wearing the ring that symbolised their marriage. In order to force a separation, she stages her knowledge of their intimate connection, only for his eyes, but in front of everyone. The straightforward plot explanation for this veiled approach is that Charlie must find discreet ways of getting rid of Charles to protect her mother. Yet this situation also enables her stately descent of the stairs while all the party awaits: she acts the bride *and* performs a solemn ceremony of separation.

When Charles arrives at the house, Emmy runs down the steps to greet him, but he tells her not to move, and she stops at the left of the frame. He stands at the right pointing at her and says 'Standing there you don't look like Emma Newton – you look like Emma Spencer Oakley of 46, Burnham Street, St Paul Minnesota, the prettiest girl on the block.' Charles' greeting is unnerving not because of its insincerity but because of its assured commitment to the sentiment. The plot explains his visit to Santa Rosa in terms of eluding the police, but he might want to get away in a deeper sense, in order to come back to himself. The vision of 46, Burnham Street is called up for himself, as much as for Emmy – 'I keep remembering all the old things' – but Cotton masks Charles' own investment to the audience, disguising it in a line that a villain might spin simply for strategy. (In later instances, the film more explicitly reveals that his psychosis is related to a perverted nostalgia, but it never discloses any specific traumatic occasion.) Cotton's pacing of his lines is careful while his vocal tone is leisurely and soothing: his voice evokes a hazy glow from the past that allows each word to be steadily warmed.

Cotton's performance remains bravely indeterminate. He avoids the easy entertainment that so many performers playing villains cannot resist. He does not play for amusement: no camping-up, sly cleverness, blatant tics, or a wink to the audience. Nor does he play the obsessive or demented weirdo: his psychotic aspects, emerging in his opinions on widows, and his bursts of anger, are reasonably infrequent and tightly contained. Even his attempts at killing Charlie are easy-going and, in line with his sartorial priorities, off the cuff. Initially lethargic – lying on his bed, money scattered carelessly around the room – he is also rather lazy in covering his tracks.[10] Although strongly committed to his world-view, he is only moderately purposeful, and is rather blasé with regard to his own plots. In film terms, he is an unusually ordinary psychopath. He is shadowy and dubious not because he slips to and from the darkness but because he is indefinite. Cotton keeps his performance impalpable creating Charles not from shadows and doubts, as many performers construct villains, but from desires subdued and indistinct – the shadows of doubts.

Charles is single-minded and nonchalant, perhaps because he is *determined* by reveries – his own and Charlie's. As one of the lead performers, Cotton's villain risks appearing indistinct but not if he is performing the insubstantial, carefully judging Charles to be a product of either his or Charlie's incompletely formed desires. On the first night of Charles' arrival, the family sits down to have dinner. Charles hands out his gifts that include a fur scarf for Emmy. Charlie says, 'it is exactly right, it is what you should have', and her delivery of the line exhibits an insistent desire for a different world under the guise of sharing her mother's pleasure at receiving an extravagant gift. 'It is exactly right' sounds like 'it suits you perfectly', but it is also the 'right' fur to match Charlie's dream, 'exactly' according with her vision of how her mother should be refurbished (she earlier showed annoyance at her mother continuing to wear a dowdy old hat in public). The scene continues with Wright acting out a dual drama.

Charlie refuses to receive a gift and runs into the kitchen where she nervously folds and fiddles with tablecloths without purpose, and as Charles enters the room, her back is turned coyly away. Like a young girl who knows the boy is about to propose, she is embarrassed and eager. Wright presents Charlie's refusal of the gift as sincere – they do not need to give presents to prove their bond – and a sexual invitation to draw him closer to committing to her.

Charles stays back against the wall near the doorway, acting the modest suitor, and the film emphasises her advance towards him, the camera retreating as she gets nearer. This is a reverse of the convention where we would view the villain's ominous approach. As she nears, she announces their strong connection: they are twinned, she knows he hides things, and these things are 'secret and wonderful.' 'We're not just an uncle and a niece', she proclaims – seemingly innocent about the innuendo of the remark. This is not a Tempting by Lolita, where the young woman's sexual aspects are prominent and pushing. Wright performs Charlie's seduction unknowingly, as if her words and movements are controlled by something beyond her reach. Indeed, despite the sexual momentum that is gathering, she remains contained in her costume. Her dress looks like a child's outfit (and she did indeed receive it some years earlier from her Uncle). Apart from the arms, very little flesh is shown. Her sexuality is hemmed in by the costume's old-fashioned trappings and corresponds to her restrictions within the traditional values of Santa Rosa. Although pulled tightly, the wide band around her middle fails to curve her figure and merely shows her waist as childishly slender. Stiffer and more angular than usual, the dress restrains her energetic movements. The large lace collar and the bow high on the neck, with thin ribbon dropping down, make it suitable for a family occasion – a communion dress perhaps. Now it acts as her bridal gown but ensures that the bride looks like a girl. She has raised, curled and fixed her hair to appear more styled and mature, but in contrast to the freer, natural look, brisk and spirited, she looks held-up and pinned back.[11]

Wright embodies these restrictions – a performer who looked and sounded more sophisticated would not carry off the aspects of an ordinary girl – while also showing a woman surrendering, barely consciously, to new compulsions. One impulse is a developing prescience for male plots. Charles says, 'Give me your hand Charlie', and she presents it palm down as if offering it to be kissed. At the same time, her gesture accords with the matrimonial ritual of the bride laying the hand on the groom's, as if she sensed she was about to receive a ring. After he places it on her finger, she backs off from him and refuses to examine it: she seems sincere in trusting that it will be beautiful and apt, and yet she also seems to be provoking him further to press her interest. Indeed, in refusing to look closely at the ring she prompts Charles to remove it and point out the emerald. It is at this point that she inspects it and sees a faint inscription: 'TS from BM.' Was she unknowingly pushing him to reveal his dangerous secrets to her? The film then presents a classic plot situation where the murderer must think on his feet to prevent the heroine's realisation, and the performer shows to us his skill in improvising truthfulness to her. The difficulty here is that Charles cannot keep control of the plot because Charlie does not respond in accord with expectations. She keeps redefining events in order to vent her vacillating urges. She delightedly says, 'You've had something engraved on it' and he replies, 'I haven't but I will if you like', perhaps hoping that she will not take a second look. She responds sharply, 'Yes you have Uncle Charlie', as if she were *wishing* to undermine him – catch him out. Should she not be pleased at his modest denial? When he says, 'I've been rooked', he calmly establishes that the jeweller has conned him, but he becomes very anxious when she says it does not matter and refuses to give it back. He demands it, and even tries to pull it from her, but his firm insistence is strangely unrecognised by her. Given her idolisation of Charles, we would expect her to be reasonable here, and return the ring to him. Yet, her desire to stubbornly hold on to it looks like a latent response to his anxiety, as if she were inviting his anger, troubling, and therefore intensifying, their *engagement*.

Beguiled that someone was once 'happy' with the ring, she is now compelled to keep a gift that only a few moments earlier she refused. Rather than reacting with suspicion, she turns the strange engraving into a marvellous mystery that supports her enchantment. At the same time, she is unwittingly taunting and unmasking him, as if the creation of her fantasy existed simultaneously with its unravelling. After saying the line, 'It's perfect the way it is', she moves back to the kitchen table, and picks up the desserts. In a forthright wifely tone she commands, 'You bring the coffee.' There is a sweep to her movement as she carries off the desserts, effectively calling an end to the scene she herself initiated after her flight from the dinner table, leaving Charles to follow. Wright melds the besotted and the contrary: self-satisfied Charlie assuredly scorns her figure of reverence.

The behaviour and motivations of the characters are multifaceted so both performers prevent us from following any single, straightforward story. They ensure that the film does not follow one plotted course. Cotton keeps his response to Charlie ambiguous: as Charles follows her out of the room his trance-like behaviour could indicate early stirrings of his murderous intent towards Charlie, but he also appears hypnotised, pulled along in *her* sweep. The film's transitions aid the performers in this regard by creating multiple relationships. The film dissolves into the nineteenth-century ballroom dancers that accompanied the opening credit sequence, and we hear 'The Merry Widow' waltz. The waltz, played by high strings, first arose on the soundtrack when Charlie announced the inscription on the ring. The playing of the waltz at this moment establishes a straightforward link between the ring and the widow murders, but less straightforwardly, the theme might also be triggered by Charlie's inspection. Moreover, although the dissolve links directly with Charles as he exits the room, and suggests this is the sequence playing in his head, it is also linked, albeit less directly, with Charlie.

The ambiguity of the associations is helped by the enigma of the dance sequence itself. Are these women widows, or are they to become widows?

Why do they look to be from another age? If the images are imagined by a character are they desired or despised, or both? During the dissolve, the theme has become more swirling, in accord with the circling dancers, and swooning, as if hummed by a choir, and when the film dissolves back into the dining room, Charlie, as if by magic, is humming the tune. (Ann says, with bizarre prescience after our witnessing of a quasi-engagement scene, that if you hum at the dinner table you marry a crazy husband!) Charlie says, 'I can't get that tune out of my head', and then proclaims, 'I think tunes jump from head to head.' She explains that, 'Sometimes I get a tune in my head like that and pretty soon I hear someone else humming it too.' Is she suggesting that the tune jumped surreptitiously without it being hummed out-loud? Is the waltz sequence playing in *her* head? Has the tune come to mind, purely by association, because the ring has triggered thoughts of widows?

The film's transitions suggest different stories simultaneously, and the performers make use of these associations. The waltz is a motif for the uncle and niece's telepathic connection, and the dissolve bleeds together Charles' walking, the 'merry widows' dancing, and Charlie's humming. Yet the precise links between these are themselves dissolved: what is the origin of the tune, in which direction is it moving, and how? The connections made by the transition suggest the mysterious psychological currents, and Wright only hints at a more serious haunting. She concentrates on presenting a picture of ordinary frustration at forgetting the origins and reasons for humming a tune. Meanwhile, the film is digging for the buried secrets that lie behind everyday frustrations and forgetfulness.

The performers use ordinary activity to suggest psychological currents, but it is not simply a means to an end. While suggesting hidden stories, Wright ensures her ordinary behaviour retains its strength and integrity. Maintaining her performance of 'ordinary eldest girl', largely unmindful of certain forces (like the performances of the 'average' family members) is crucial because it shows the repetitions of the everyday to have extraordinary resilience. They are not easily disturbed, and Charles' plots cannot easily defeat them. Indeed, undramatic aspects of Newton household behaviour – a burst of humming while fetching the plates and a dinnertime discussion about remembering the tune – dangerously threaten to expose Uncle Charles (he knocks over a glass and creates a spillage to interrupt proceedings). In the next scene, Charles has moved into the front room where Emmy has given him the newspaper to read. In the newspaper, he sees an incriminating story about the murders, and needs to dispose of the crucial page. He calls Ann over, and shows her how to make a house out of newspaper. He remains seated and she stands over him, making the best efforts to hide her impatience: she sighs just a little, and restrains her fidgeting to a slight sway. With a mixture of politeness and resoluteness, she stays and watches obediently until he finishes. Then, not a moment too soon, urgently tells him that she is not a baby anymore and besides this is 'poppa's paper'. Her precociousness is in tension with her unwillingness to be rude and her attentiveness to her father's habits. As youngest son Roger (Charles Bates) enters, Charles tries to bring him into the cover-up, but he marches over and indignantly announces, 'You've got poppa's paper.' Roger outstretches his arm to point at the crime, and the shot moves hurriedly in the direction of his gesture to the mess of papers lying on the floor. The rush of movement matches the sense of an uncontrollable upsurge in the boy's feelings. An everyday ritual – father religiously reading his paper – is dramatically evoked through a traumatic disturbance to it.

The scene is delightfully droll, because there are no deliberate intentions to thwart the villain; Charles tries in vain to straighten out the plot, but succeeds only in the calamity of messing up 'poppa's paper.' The viewer knows what Charles is up to, the child performers know what he is up to, but they play a wonderful game of pretend, presenting a performance of unwavering dedication. In doing so, they show Ann and Roger to have respect for their father's everyday life, but also to be in awe of it – in the grip of the daily rounds. Without description or elaboration, they conjure a picture of father sitting reading his paper after work everyday. The young performers enact a simple piece of child behaviour, and give us a vision of an adult life. Finally, Charlie enters and declares, 'What are you two doing? You know that is your father's paper', and without thinking she adopts the role of a mother: still dressed in her old-fashioned frock, she tells off the kids, and kneels on the floor to put

things right. On her knees, she presents a potent image of the power of the ordinary to reassert itself: pulled into saving the daily paper, she is frantically forced into protecting the everyday that she was eager to reject. Wright adopts the role efficiently and automatically, and illustrates in a moment how a woman of this background, despite temporary resistances, instinctively moves into a domestic position.

There is a crucial tension in *Shadow of a Doubt*, therefore, between the explicit stories which characters try to control (for example, Charlie unmasking Charles, Charles preventing disclosure) and the stories that are controlling them. The performers have the challenge of performing these, often contradictory, stories simultaneously. Given the circumstances with 'poppa's paper', Charlie slips almost unwittingly into a motherly role. Earlier, in the kitchen, she played the feisty bride-to-be, necessarily controlling the terms upon which she would submit. Later that night she excitedly intends to find out the secret in the newspaper, but she is consumed by another role, that of the sexually eager virgin.

The sequence might be viewed as the performers simply but effectively progressing the plot. She stands at the bedroom doorway while he sits at the far end of the room in an armchair polishing his shoes. Her eyes catch sight of his jacket pocket, hanging over a nearby chair, where the incriminating newspaper page is folded up and sticking out. She shuts the door quietly so that he cannot make a quick departure and so no one else will hear the revelations. She taunts him about knowing his 'secret' and says she knows there was something in the evening paper. He makes up an excuse, but she grabs it. Then from her perspective, we see him urgently rising and marching over, eventually looming, and gripping her wrists. The plot explanation for this violent outburst is straightforward – he is an unhinged killer – and a lazy film with complacent performers would have settled for the cheap thrill of the incident. *Why does she not realise? Will he hurt her? Will it be too late?*

Wright and Cotton, however, perform it like lovemaking, with passion bleeding uncomfortably into violence. By slyly shutting the door with her arms behind her back while she holds her flirtatious stare, she also looks to be protecting their intimacy, indicating that now is the time to make love. This might be the posture of an experienced seductress, were it not for her wide-eyed, virginal innocence. She touches his secrets. He rises and takes hold of her. He is on top. She says, 'You're hurting me', but this is not surprising, after all, this is her first time. Of course, having had his wicked way, he says, 'I didn't mean to hurt you, I was just fooling.' She immediately surrenders to the man's apology, in just the way a young girl should. He pulls her closer as if he is about to kiss her and she looks up into his eyes, fluttering her lids, under his spell. Then she smiles and sighs, melting into the lovers' embrace (he now holds each upper arm). She realises that her fear was merely nervousness before losing her virginity. This is how it should be. He puts his hand softly on her cheek. With the door now open, she backs out of the room, refusing to break eye contact. Only when she is far enough away do their outstretched arms stop touching; having made love, they cannot bear to separate. Her hand strokes the frame of the door and she slides away looking back at him captivated. Considering she was assaulted only a few seconds earlier, Wright is worryingly quick and convincing at moving into this state of rapture. Cotton's performance of unawareness is equally perturbing, for although Charles means violently to wrestle back control from Charlie, he too seems innocent, or unaware, of the sexual developments. They both unwittingly take up all the sexual positions, and even when separated the pattern continues. They are both lying on their backs in bed – mirroring their own mirroring at the beginning of the film – and Charles, suitably post-coital, is smoking.

Celia and Charlie's stories may be therapeutic dreams (or nightmares), but this is not something the films confirm. Reality and fantasy are indistinguishable because the style of performance remains consistent (as do the status of the image and the tone of the drama). Similarly, by credibly and clearly acting out the central plot – precisely establishing its strength and direction – the performers simultaneously challenge its authority. They embrace its linearity to create other dimensions, seamlessly, so that straightforward narratives become worlds.

A FINAL WORD

Although performers often guide our viewing of films, we find it difficult to articulate our appreciation. Instead we become diverted, and tend to talk or write about the characters in films without acknowledging their *presence* as human figures. Despite its focus on movement, posture and gesture, however, this study has not tried to distil a performer's physique or expressions, or even their manner more generally, in odd words, or a couple of sentences. There are critics – Manny Farber, David Thomson and Raymond Durgnat – who have shown a talent for succinctly capturing the essence of a performer. This study has presented a method for sustaining attention to a *performance*, and has appreciated the achievement of performance in ten films from the 'Golden Age' of Hollywood.

Concentrating on a sequence or a succession of sequences from each film (rather than ranging across examples from within the films, or between several films of a specific performer) directs our attention to the moment-by-moment development of the performances. It enables an exploration of the tight-knit relationship of the performances to the surrounding aspects of film style. Continuous attention to sequences also brings out the relationship between appreciating a performance and understanding a film's meaning as it *develops* – the unfolding of an interpretation – undermining our inclination to condense and compress meanings of films, often to the point of banality. Established understandings may then be substantially deepened – or unseated. This method also requires that we slow down, stop, and dwell, so that we can savour the intensity of an interaction, an intonation or an expression – the reverberations – and reflect (on) the resonance.

In addition, the uninterrupted perspective permits a prose based on description. Outside the Introduction, and this Final Word, and occasional summarising remarks throughout, the book avoids the common method of film study where extended explanation or theorisation is articulated separately from the works (and sometimes replaces the works). Instead, conceptualisation and interpretation are internal to the critical process of depiction. The prose endeavours to evoke the films and interpret them at the same time. Understandings of performance emerge simultaneously during an account of what happens on the screen. The purpose of this, rather than simply attempting a more expressive prose, is to reflect the manner of the films where what they mean *is* what they are and what they do. They do not provide separate explanations of themselves. (Despite wishing to illuminate the sequences, and make sense of them, this study also wishes to respect their mystery and suggestiveness.)

Throughout, this book reiterates the achievement of rapport. This achievement may be found in many films other than those from the 'Golden Age' of Hollywood, and the method of analysis should be useful beyond this particular context. Yet it is during this period that we recurrently see it manifested. One quality, at least, connects the performances discussed here: their awareness and responsiveness to the aspects that surround them, and the *thoroughness* of their interaction. The performers do not take the easy route, eagerly moving from one point to the next, although it is tempting in this narrative art. Their achievement is to devote themselves to the film's world. Restricted to a street corner and a shop window, Charlie Chaplin twists and turns around many moods. As long as they have each other, a piano or a sofa are all Stan Laurel and Oliver Hardy need for creative variation and elaboration. Irene Dunne and Cary Grant repeatedly play with the same words to mean different things while the same faulty door generates different outcomes. Cary Grant positions himself patiently so he may nudge the participants in Philadelphia through various arrangements and into happy consequences. Marlene Dietrich transforms herself, magisterially, by stroking the nooks and crannies of the Russian palace. Fred MacMurray hovers in the in-between spaces of his house – the landing, the stairs and the walk-in washroom – and reveals his 'mid-life' inertia. While everyone passes him by, or runs around him, Barbara Stanwyck has the intensity and generosity to stop, look, and revivify everything around him. Richard Widmark endeavours to find a comfortable place to sit in a variety of households. Joan Bennett and Theresa Wright respond keenly to each inkling and intimation so their stories are successfully therapeutic. Yet the appreciation of all these performers depends on our own concentration because the acuity of their attentiveness is belied by the ease of their integration.

NOTES

introduction

1 Whereas one might unpack the density of *mise-ên-scène* in appraising the films of Orson Welles, Max Ophüls, Fritz Lang, Alfred Hitchcock, Douglas Sirk and others there is a critical difficulty in assessing the quality of the comparably 'thin' *mise-ên-scène* in the films of Charles Chaplin, Laurel and Hardy, George Cukor and Leo McCarey (who indeed directed some Laurel and Hardy films).

chapter one

1 William Rothman muses on this axis, and other aspects of the scene, as a meditation on the film medium. His discussion inspired this section of the chapter (see Rothman 1988: 48–60).
2 Detractors of Chaplin's work who charge him with succumbing to obvious sentiment might note this.
3 There are some unfortunate continuity errors at this point. Chaplin's hand and the flower keep shifting positions between the edits.
4 I have elsewhere characterised Laurel and Hardy's behaviour as expressing the inevitable need for, and yet the difficulties of, human relatedness in the middle of the desperate endeavour to stay devoted to the world of one's life (Klevan 2000: 26).
5 'Her wriggles underneath the blanket act as a teasing taunt and an undis-

closed promise, a suggestion of feisty sexuality – albeit under the covers. Her handling of the blanket shrouds her body (makes her bodiless), and ... will provoke the thrill of its rediscovery.' This comes from a previous discussion of the scene and its relationship to repetition and the ordinary (Klevan 2000: 27).

6 For a penetrating discussion of Cary Grant's capacity to 'play' see Andrew Britton (1986).
7 The Shakespearean connection is explored by Stanley Cavell (1981).
8 For Cavell, conversation is a crucial component in the 'Comedies of Remarriage' and *The Awful Truth* and *The Philadelphia Story* are members of this grouping.

chapter two

1 Thank you to Amy Allen for her illuminating comments on this gesture.

chapter three

1 Most readings of the film seem to also revolve around this concern. See, for example, Michael Walker (1990).
2 Two other important instances of this (sub-)genre are *Rebecca* (Alfred Hitchcock, 1940) and *Gaslight* (George Cukor, 1944).
3 See George M. Wilson (1986) for a discussion of the strategies by which another Lang film, *You Only Live Once* (US, 1937), tells simultaneously credible stories. Lang's films engage especially in these strategies, but Wilson's book *Narration in Light* understands it to be a possible quality of any good film – to tell simultaneous stories while appearing not to – and we should be alert to this. See also Klevan (2003).
4 Thank you to Alan Jones for refining my understanding of this part of the film.
5 Mary Ann Doane tantalisingly suggests that 'what the woman confronts on the other side of the door is an aspect of herself' (1989: 137) but Doane does not explore the consequences of this remark for Celia's self-realisation. She also concludes that after the fade-out the 'remainder of the narrative is devoted to the psychoanalysis of Mark, to the attempt to open the 'locked door' of his mind ... the void on the image track gives witness to ... the death of female subjectivity' (1989: 151). Tom Gunning rightly takes issue with this

and suggests that, 'Far from losing her voice, Celia has learned to speak.' Despite pointing this out, Gunning still focuses 'squarely' on the psychosis of Mark, going on to say that she has 'located her problem no longer in fear ... but squarely in her husband' (2002: 360).

6 With the exception of pointing violently at Mark when she forces him to face his demons!

7 Thank you to David Turner for encouraging me to think about aspects of symmetry in the film.

8 William Rothman's account of the film in his book *Hitchcock – The Murderous Gaze* (1982) is pressing and perspicacious about the role of (Hitchcock's) camera within the fiction.

9 A distinction made by Raymond Durgnat (1974: 183).

10 Raymond Durgnat (1974: 186) discusses his apathy, and stimulated these observations.

11 Thank you to Lucy Fife for her imaginative insights on costume.

BIBLIOGRAPHY

Affron, C. (1977) *Star Acting: Gish, Garbo, Davis*. New York: E. P. Dutton.

Britton, A. (1986) 'Cary Grant: Comedy and Male Desire', *Cineaction*, 7, December, 36–51.

Cavell, S. (1979) *The World Viewed: Reflections on the Ontology of Film (enlarged edition)*. Cambridge and London: Harvard University Press.

____ (1981) *Pursuits of Happiness: The Hollywood Comedy of Remarriage*. Cambridge and London: Harvard University Press.

____ (1996) *Contesting Tears: The Hollywood Melodrama of the Unknown Woman*. Chicago and London: University of Chicago Press.

DiBattista, M. (2001) *Fast-Talking Dames*. New Haven and London: Yale University Press.

Doane, M. A. (1988) *The Desire to Desire: The Woman's Film of the 1940s*. London: MacMillan.

Durgnat, R. (1967) *Films and Feelings*. London: Faber and Faber.

____ (1974) *The Strange Case of Alfred Hitchcock*. London: Faber and Faber.

Harvey, J. (1998) *Romantic Comedy in Hollywood: From Lubitsch to Sturges*. New York: De Capo Press.

Keane, M. (1993) 'Dyer Straits: Theoretical Issues in Studies of Film Acting', *Postscipt*, 12, 2, 29–39.

Klevan, A. (1999) 'The Composition of Charisma: The Lines of Sporting Seduction in Ron Shelton's *Tin Cup*', *Film Studies*, 1, Spring, 51–62.

____ (2000) *Disclosure of the Everyday: Undramatic Achievement in Narrative Film*. Trowbrige: Flicks Books.

____ (2003) 'The Purpose of Plot and the Place of Joan Bennett in Fritz Lang's *The Woman in the Window*', *Cineaction*, 62, December, 15–21.

____ (2005a) 'Guessing the Unseen from the Seen: Stanley Cavell and Film Interpretation', in R. Goodman (ed.) *Contending with Stanley Cavell*. Oxford: Oxford University Press, 256–95.

____ (2005b) 'Notes on Teaching Film Style', in J. Gibbs and D. Pye (eds) *Style and Meaning*. Manchester: Manchester University Press, 214–27.

Naremore, J. (1988) *Acting in the Cinema*. Los Angeles and London: University of California Press.

Paglia, C. (1998) *The Birds*. London: British Film Institute.

Perkins, V. F. (1972; reprinted 1991) *Film as Film: Understanding and Judging Movies*. London: Penguin.

____ (1999) *The Magnificent Ambersons*. London: British Film Institute.

Rothman, W. (1982) *Hitchcock: The Murderous Gaze*. Cambridge: Cambridge University Press.

____ (1989) *The 'I' of the Camera*. Cambridge and New York: Cambridge University Press.

Stern, L. and Kouvaros, G. (eds) (1999) *Falling For You: Essays on Cinema and Performance*. Sydney: Power Publications.

Thomson, D. (1967) *Movie Man*. New York: Stein and Day.

____ (1975; reprinted 1994) *A Biographical Dictionary of the Cinema*. London: Andre Deutsch.

Walker, M. (1990) '*Secret Beyond the Door*', *Movie*, 34/35, 16–30.

Wilson, G. M. (1986) *Narration in Light: Studies in Cinematic Point of View*. Baltimore and London: Johns Hopkins University Press.

Wood, R. (1976) *Personal Views*. London: G. Fraser.

____ (1976) 'Acting Up', *Film Comment*, 12, 2, 20–5.

Zucker, C. (ed.) (1990) *Making Visible the Invisible: An Anthology of Original Essays on Film Acting*. Metuchen, NJ and London: Scarecrow Press.

INDEX

The Hollywood Story

Joel Finler

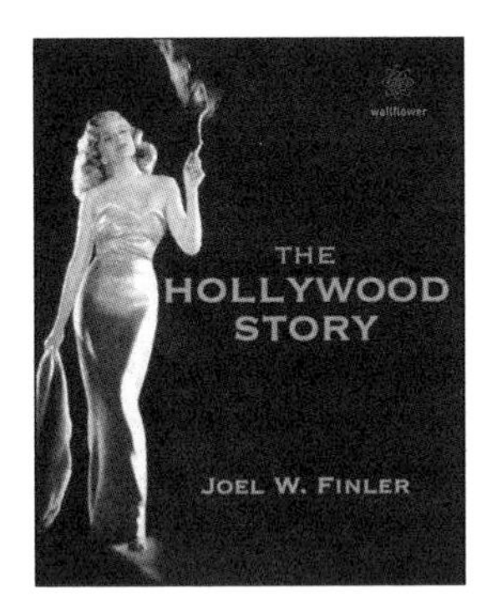

2003
£16.99 pbk
1-903364-66-3

In *The Hollywood Story*, Joel W. Finler explores the history of the American movie industry from the silent era up to the present day. In individual chapters that cover each of the major studios, the author considers the key actors, directors and frequently overlooked technicians who contributed to filmmaking history. The book includes a wealth of information on the development of colour, wide-screen processes and the transition from silent cinema to sound. Additionally, Joel W. Finler has compiled an unrivalled amount of financial information which is presented in simple graphs and tables, making it clearer than ever just what, and who, are the big winners and losers in Hollywood.

The Hollywood Story won the British Film Institute award as the outstanding film book of 1989. This fully revised and updated edition brings the facts and figures into the new millennium and includes an entirely new chapter on the studio that emerged in the 1990s as one of the most powerful of all – Disney.

'Pride of place must go to Joel W. Finler's *The Hollywood Story* which purports to be 'everything you always wanted to know about the American movie business but didn't know where to look' and actually delivers ... the writing is clear and unpretentious and the whole thing is a work of persistent scholarship ... well produced and well presented too.'
– Derek Malcolm, *The Guardian*

'An absolute must for anyone interested in the studio system ... Finler has written an absorbing *aide memoire* for buffs and fans alike.'
– Clive Hirschhorn, *Sunday Express*

'*The Hollywood Story* is a must for the movie buff ... Never has so much information been compiled into one easy-to-read accessible volume.'
– Bob Dorian, *American Movie Classics*

'A book that more than lives up to its claims ... For all those unable to store sixty years of *Variety* under the bed, Mr Finler has performed an invaluable service.'
– *The Economist*